What the Underground Church in China Is Saying About *I Stand with Christ*

This is unlike most book endorsement sections, which are filled with affirmations from scholars or famous pastors and preachers. You may not recognize the following names, but they are among the most respected leaders of the Chinese underground house church. Together, their churches represent more than seventy million believers throughout China.

～

As I read this book, I cried until I finished it. Once I picked it up, I could not put it down. I consumed it in one day. I was shocked at the kind of witness Pastor Zhang Rongliang has been for the Lord. Instead of touching the lives of just a few people, God has used him to touch the lives of millions all across China.

Those who heard the messages preached by Zhang Rongliang ended up surrendering their lives, picking up the cross, and following Jesus. As I read this book and thought about the people involved with Pastor Zhang, I had to stop and ask myself, "What kind of people are these?" These people are crazy. They willingly give up their own freedom and comfortable lives to take on a life of persecution and hardship. These are not normal people. Normal people do not do the things that are found in this book. Normal people just want to have a family, live their lives in comfort, and have good health.

Again, as I read this book, I was not able to hold back my emotion. On one side, I appreciate how God's rescue and mercy continued throughout the challenging times of China's early years, but on the other side, I want to pray that God will keep His ch̶u̶r̶c̶h̶ ̶p̶r̶o̶t̶e̶c̶t̶e̶d̶ ̶f̶r̶o̶m̶ ̶p̶e̶r̶s̶e̶c̶u̶t̶i̶on. This story of Zhang should remind u̶s̶ ̶ e life is, we should never forget the lesson̶ ̶ secution have always been with the churc̶ ̶ ch truly follows in the footsteps of Jesus, u̶ ̶ ery early disciple had to learn this lesson, and many met death in the glorious fires of persecution.

So what is our responsibility today? I think that this book makes us ask if we are truly willing to suffer for the Lord. It compels us to ask if we are truly willing to give our lives for Him as He did for us. Around the world today, there are many Christians who are suffering and being tortured for Jesus Christ with the hopes of one day being reunited with our heavenly Father. That is what this book reminds us of.

I Stand with Christ describes the deepest details of Pastor Zhang's life. Maybe, like me, you will not be able to hold back your tears as you read this story. My heart was revived and my spiritual life was challenged after reading this book. My prayer is that Pastor Zhang will never again suffer from the pain of chains, shackles, whips, or starvation in prison but instead fly like an eagle until the Lord calls him home.

—*Xiao Min*
Singer and songwriter for the underground house church

I view Pastor Zhang Rongliang as an outstanding and respected leader in the Chinese underground church. We have had more than thirty years of serving together. Through the years, we have had some disagreements, but the love that we share keeps us working together in Christ. Together, we have been in the same boat of persecution, faced the same storms, and faced suffering together.

I am so glad to witness his story finally being told in this long-awaited autobiography. Pastor Zhang has witnessed God's leading hand of protection at every turn of his life. His story is not about him alone but is the story of the Fangcheng underground house church—one of China's largest house church networks. If you read Pastor Zhang's story, you will also learn the details of the last forty years of history in China's church.

Pastor Zhang's story is one that brings glory and praise to God, because we can witness how the faithful rely upon God during the hardest times in life. My hope is that this book will bring revival and encouragement for brothers and sisters around the world and leave an eternal spiritual blessing for the church of Jesus Christ.

—*Pastor Chen Xiao Fu*
Beijing

When I finished reading the story about Zhang Rongliang, I immediately felt that this is a book that all pastors should read. This is not just the experience of one pastor but also the story of the underground church in China. The last sixty years of China's church history can be better understood by reading *I Stand with Christ*. There are so many things about the underground house church that are not known to the rest of the world, but Pastor Zhang's personal testimony fills in the blanks. I am so thankful for this book.

Zhang Rongliang's life is full of miraculous marvels that come as the result of relying upon Jesus. From begging for food, to tending sheep, to being a member of the Communist Party, to being thrown in prison for the gospel, we see it all. As we say in China, we are able to follow his life from black hair to white hair.

God has always been with Pastor Zhang and rescued him during times of trouble. It is impossible to imagine China's revival of the Holy Spirit without Pastor Zhang. His testimony and witness proves that Jesus is alive and is not dead. Jesus is living in Chinese hearts far and wide throughout China.

Just as Jesus whispered to Peter, He also whispered to Pastor Zhang, "If you love me, feed my sheep."

—*Pastor Zhen Ju Xing*
Shenzhen

My dear brother Pastor Zhang Rongliang, who is a big influence in China, suffered and shared trials in Jesus Christ. I am happy that he has written this book because it shares a sober story of God's love. Pastor Zhang comes from Fangcheng in Henan Province, but I come from Zhe Jiang Province, so we didn't meet until early 1981. Going back in my memory, I am reminded of the messages that I heard Pastor Zhang preach with passion, like the ones that he preached at a secret gathering during Chinese Spring Festival in 1982.

During those early days, to the outside observer, it seemed that the house church was being broken down and torn apart by persecution, but on the inside, the church was only getting stronger. During the most trying times, Pastor Zhang's messages brought power and encouragement—not just to his church in Fangcheng but to all of China's underground house churches. His influence cannot be underestimated.

He is a remarkable leader. The amazing story that he shares in this book shows how he led one of most well-known churches in China. I know many of these stories personally because I was there. Between 1982–1986, I had a lot chances to visit with the underground church in Fangcheng. Whether it was summer or winter, hot or cold, busy or not, Pastor Zhang was always able to gather coworkers and evangelists to study and train. He always preached a fiery message encouraging us to lay down our lives and obey God's Word. I saw the church grow through an amazing revival during those years. The gospel was preached so widely and quickly throughout China because of those messages. Pastor Zhang was able to build up and send out teams, and he played a pivotal part in setting the foundation for the big five house church networks.

From personally observing the life of Pastor Zhang, I can say that I understand better what it is to be a servant of God. I saw the power of the Holy Spirit introduced in Henan during the early days of the church, and all of the brothers and sisters who felt dry and thirsty were able to be filled with the Holy Spirit. Pastor Zhang, together with Pastor Dennis Balcombe, played a key role in this outpouring. By obeying God's leading in his life, Pastor Zhang was able to see much fruit. Not only did his church rise in membership under his leadership, but some of the members eventually gave their lives in martyrdom for the gospel.

The fire that God put in Pastor Zhang was not able to be quenched. It was not extinguished by persecution, prison, or threat of death. Even though he was persecuted by the government and thrown in prison numerous times, the enemy could not stop him. I believe that it was only through the power of the Holy Spirit that so many millions of people came to believe in Jesus Christ through the vessel of Pastor Zhang, who willingly gave himself in submission to the Spirit. Today, Pastor Zhang's main mission is to take the gospel to the rest of the world between China and Jerusalem in what is known as the "Back to Jerusalem" vision. His voice is among those voices encouraging the church to fulfill the Great Commission.

The journey of the Chinese church has been from chaos to order, from no framework to framework, and from hardship to revival. The church has grown, but not without challenges. There have been disagreements, splits, and conflict, but Pastor Zhang continues to march on, leading the church from cold to hot. I have never met anyone with a heart as big as Pastor Zhang's. He has shown patience and has lived life by biblical principles. I have seen him solve conflicts within the church and combat heresy with amazingly tactful wisdom. Pastor Zhang was the man that God used to bring His revival to China. My prayers are with him until the Lord returns again.

—*Pastor Peter Xu*
USA

Pastor Zhang is both noble and precious and has been greatly used by God. My heart was deeply moved when I read his testimony. It reminded me of the stories that were recorded in the film *The Cross* about the underground church in China. He is like a blooming flower that sprouted during China's spiritual spring. His flower brought beauty to China during a time when everything was dark and grey. As I read his testimony, I found myself crying, laughing, and remembering. You see, Pastor Zhang represents all of us simple farmer Christians in China today. We are not educated; we are simple, but we are loyal. Our loyalty has brought us to a place where we are willing to die for the sake of the cross.

When I read the part about Pastor Zhang demanding that his mother give the shoes back to the government, even though he didn't have any shoes, I found myself laughing because I know him and I can actually see the scene in my mind's eye. Pastor Zhang was not released from prison until recently, and my hope is that his tears of sorrow from the persecution that he endured will be turned to shouts of joy.

—*Pastor Yuan Zhi Ming*

I STAND WITH CHRIST

I STAND WITH CHRIST

THE COURAGEOUS LIFE OF A CHINESE CHRISTIAN

ZHANG RONGLIANG WITH EUGENE BACH

WHITAKER
HOUSE

I STAND WITH CHRIST:
The Courageous Life of a Chinese Christian

Back to Jerusalem, Inc.
www.backtojerusalem.com

ISBN: 978-1-62911-337-1
eBook ISBN: 978-1-62911-338-8
Printed in the United States of America
© 2015 by Back to Jerusalem, Inc.

Whitaker House
1030 Hunt Valley Circle
New Kensington, PA 15068
www.whitakerhouse.com

6 7 8 9 10   ₩   21 20 19 18 17

Contents

Acknowledgments

Brother Stone: Over a period of more than two years, Brother Stone videotaped tens of hours of testimony and stories as Pastor Zhang went back and searched the furthest parts of his memory. This enabled Pastor Zhang's words to be played over and over so they could be correctly interpreted. Without Brother Stone, this book would not have been possible. He developed a friendship and familiarity with Pastor Zhang that allowed him to share the most intimate parts of his life with the rest of the world.

Brother Zhu: He took time out of his demanding schedule of completing his doctorate to fly to China and get the outline and timeline for Pastor Zhang's life. He used his amazing gift of research to set the tone of this book so that it truly reflects the events of Pastor Zhang's life.

Back to Jerusalem, Inc.: They financially invested in this story so that it could be told. Without the backing of Back to Jerusalem, Inc., it would not have been possible to arrange for the countless expenses of travel, plane tickets, hotel rooms, etc., to make this book possible. Back to Jerusalem wanted to invest in this book to bless the life of Pastor Zhang. One hundred percent of all royalties of this book by the publisher go to Pastor Zhang.

Bob Whitaker: He personally involved himself to assist the church in China. After a short afternoon meeting with me over lunch at Ruby Tuesday, Bob put all of the resources of Whitaker House behind the efforts of the underground house church in China to support its vision— including Pastor Zhang's testimony. He and his friends at Whitaker

House brought a level of exposure and professionalism to Pastor Zhang's story that otherwise would never have happened. He has been more than a partner—he has been a dear friend to the persecuted church in China.

Dr. Roberts Liardon: He and his friend Don Milam used their various contacts and expert advice for the direction needed to get this book published. Both of these men used selfless acts of Christian-motivated devotion to ensure that the history of one of the most important Chinese underground house church pastors would be told.

Lois Puglisi: The hardest job regarding anything that I write is the editing stage. Lois has exercised so much grace, patience, and devotion when working with me and editing this book. She has become someone that I have come to rely on greatly in the last two years to take a roughly written story and turn it into something that is amazing. She does so much more than correct grammar and spelling. She somehow finds a way to take awkward sentences and ideas and arrange them so that they effectively communicate with passion to the reader.

—*Eugene Bach*

Foreword

I am Brother Yun, "the Heavenly Man." For the sake of the gospel, I have shared much persecution together with Pastor Zhang Rongliang. I was put in prison for more than thirteen years of my life, but by the power of Jesus Christ, I was able to persevere.

I am so excited about Zhang Rongliang's testimony being shared with the world and feel humbled that I can write something about this book. Pastor Zhang and I share a long history. We have been arrested together, we have become homeless together, and we have walked through the lowest valley and up to the highest peaks together. We have also shared many moments of joy and laughter.

Both of us are products of the underground house church in China, and both of us were elders of the Sinim Fellowship—a fellowship of underground house church networks. After reading just a few pages of Zhang's personal story, I was so moved. I could not help but stop reading and get down on my knees to pray to God. Immediately, I shouted in prayer, "For the cross, for the cross—it is all for the glory of the cross. Forever may God help us to preach to the nations!"

My heart was deeply and profoundly moved as I continued to read *I Stand with Christ*. My heart filled with a deep fear to ensure that all thanks goes to God. The night that I first started to read this book, I immediately devoured it, reading from chapter to chapter. What I was reading was satisfying me as if I was eating a filling meal. I read the story throughout the night and really felt that I was reading David's psalms. When I finally looked up from the book, I saw that the night had passed; it was already dawn.

Thanks to our God who chooses us. We do not have a thing to boast about. We are all full of weaknesses, shortcomings, failures, and offenses. Pastor Zhang and I have our weaknesses, but we are serving God before the angels of heaven. It is only because of the blood of Jesus that we are able to play our part. It is our responsibility to witness His faithful message of power and righteousness.

I highly recommend this book with great prayer and blessing. I believe that Pastor Zhang's life story is a powerful testimony of the cross that will impact both the church in the West and the church in the East. On the way back to Jerusalem, the Father is looking for His sons and daughters to turn their hearts to Him. If we turn to Him, He will turn to us. I wish that the church today could return to the days of the apostles, that believers would be ready to lay down their lives for God with boldness, as Pastor Zhang has done. Let us read this story and be reminded that we are to continue preaching the good news to every nation, tribe, and tongue until everyone has had a chance to hear.

—*Brother Yun*
Author, *The Heavenly Man*

PROLOGUE:

My Testimony Belongs to Christ

My name is Zhang Rongliang, and I am an unashamed follower of Jesus Christ. I am the pastor of a little countryside church known as Fangcheng. I don't really know how many people are in our humble church, but most international sources estimate it to be a fellowship of about ten million believers. Some say that the numbers are much less than that, and others that it could be more. Only God truly knows the number. I don't think it really matters.

In these pages, I want to share with you my personal testimony as given to me by the Lord. It is considered quite dangerous to reveal the contents of this book, but these are stories that need to be told for God's glory and for the encouragement of the church. I spent a period of many months working on this book with international authors who traveled to China and sat down with me, painstakingly going over each part of my story. It was not an easy task, and many times, my throat became parched or my eyes became wet with tears of remembrance. My life story is complicated and full of ups and downs. I have been arrested and thrown in jail several times; I have spent a large portion of my life behind bars, serving five separate prison sentences.

I count it a privilege to have suffered for the name of my Lord Jesus Christ. Through all the lonely nights and hopeless situations, He has never left me nor forsaken me.

This story is not really mine to share. I believe that my life is not my own, and thus my testimony is not my own but rather belongs to Christ. He alone saved me and redeemed me. All that I have and all that I can tell about my life belongs to Him. I desire to be like one who is dead so that Christ can live through me, and that is why I am telling this story. I want to share about His never-ending love, His never-ending grace, and His never-failing companionship.

1

The Great Leap Forward

I was born on March 23, 1951, to an extremely poor family in Fangcheng County, Henan Province, during one of the most difficult times in China's long history. I am the middle child, my older sister now being seventy-three and my younger sister fifty-seven. My father worked as a carpenter and used his craftsmanship as best he could to provide for the needs of all our family members. However, there were still times when we had little food and had to search the fields to look for wild vegetables. My older sister could bear hunger, but my younger sister and I cried all day and begged our mother for food. Our mother loved us more than she loved herself, and one day, as we were crying again from hunger, she said, "My dear children, please don't cry! Mommy knows that you are very hungry, but every time you cry, my heart aches even more." My younger sister and I seemed to understand our mother's pain, so we stopped crying and learned to endure.

In 1956, my parents took me to the town of Lushan, then down to Nanyang and Zhenping, to beg for food. All of us would go door-to-door as we begged. My father would often offer to trade his carpentry skills for food if there was any work to be done or any food to be earned. Some people were quite unfriendly and could not understand why we were going around asking for food. Sometimes, we would find people who would share with us, but just about everyone during those days was poor and didn't have a lot of food to give to others. Starvation was rampant; it was common for us to see the bodies of those who had died of hunger lying in the street.

Our family had to fight to survive, and we would travel around all day looking for food, often only being able to scrape together two bowls of rice to feed the whole family. For two years, we had to beg for food every day because it was the only way we could stay alive. Now, as I look back on those years, I feel that a child should never have to beg for food. The constant rejection and uncertainty were not easy to deal with, and they have left their mark on me to this day. Those were terrible, painful years for me.

Then China implemented a nationwide law requiring multiple households to share the same cooking pot, meaning that we were able to share some of our neighbors' food. It was not much, but we no longer had to beg to survive. During the "The Great Leap Forward" (1958–1961), a disastrous attempt by the Communist Party to modernize the nation, there were very few pots available for cooking because everyone had been forced to give up their pots in 1958–1959 to contribute to the nation's steel production. Chairman Mao believed that steel production was the true representation of a superpower. He wanted to surpass England and America in the production of steel so that China could take its rightful place as a global force. As a result, our village had only one pot for 250 households to use. And things were so bad that we were able to get noodles only once every seven or eight days. Those familiar with Henan Province know that noodles are the staple food for the local people.

For two years, we had to beg for food every day because it was the only way we could stay alive.

By 1960, we were feeling the full effect of the Great Leap Forward policies and found ourselves on the margin of death. All of China was enduring a crisis at the time. From 1958 to 1962, China experienced what turned out to be the largest famine in the history of the world. Through its programs, the government had created a man-made disaster that killed an estimated forty-five million people over four years, not only through starvation, but also through beatings, torture, or being worked to death. Chairman Mao Zedong (Tse-tung), considered to be the father of Communist China after taking over in 1949, was in power then. The chairman mocked reports of famine in the country and denied that there was a food crisis, calling it merely a "period of scarcity." During that time, some collectives or communes were divided into groups. Food was distributed according to one's capacity for work. The elderly, the weak, and the handicapped quickly perished under this scheme.

Rural China was hit the hardest by the famine. Many families tried to make broth out of anything they could find, including tree bark. The government confiscated livestock from farmers to "serve the greater good," only to waste it and allow it to rot at the hands of inexperienced urbanites and cadre members. Painful stories from those days include those of children who were too weak to cry and were left to die in empty fields. Suicide was epidemic. More than one million people died by taking their own lives.

My own father was among the millions who perished during those years. In February 1960, he died of starvation, and my mother was left to take care of us by herself. My father just lay down to sleep one day and never got up. Even though I was nine years old at the time, I don't remember much about the event, perhaps because I didn't witness his death. My mother simply told me that my father was no longer with us. With so much starvation all around us, we knew it would inevitably happen to us all.

I kept thinking that my father would come back to life. It didn't seem real that he would no longer be with us every day. I kept expecting to hear his voice coming from around the corner or for him to come to our room and get us ready for bed. I waited for him to return, but he never did. Since I was only a child, the idea of death was not easy for me to grasp. I didn't have much knowledge about death at the time, even though it was occurring all around me. As time went on, I became very familiar with death, and I have tasted of it more times than I wish to remember.

All of China was on a downhill trajectory at that time, but as a child I didn't understand the meaning or the cause of it. I knew only that I was hungry and that my mother worked hard to find enough food to feed her children. Every day seemed to be a new struggle just to keep alive. We lived in a village of about two hundred thousand people called Longchuan (Yangji today). Our house was a small hut made of mud, clay, and grass.

We shared our hut with three other families, and there was a small, dark room in the corner of the house where we would all sleep on the dirt floor. I can still clearly remember how my mother, like a mother hen, would prepare a place for her children to sleep on the floor late in the evening.

My mother was often tired from days filled with work and worry. She was extremely undernourished, and her skin barely covered her bony frame. She would give any extra food she had to us instead of eating it herself. I remember being able to see the outline of her body even in the darkness of the room at night as she prepared to lie down.

Even though all of China was suffering, our village stood out as a place that was in a serious state of crisis.

During those years, my mother fought with death every day. I think that she would have warmly greeted death if she hadn't had us children to take care of. She had watched my father go to sleep and never wake up, and she feared the same would happen to us. At one point, my older sister married, so it was just my younger sister and me in the house. I believe that my mother's love for us and her dedication to provide for and take care of us kept her alive day after day.

Every night, she would lie down beside me and gaze at me as if she were looking at me for the last time. Her voice would break through the silence as she said, "My son, I have taken off my shoes tonight, but when the morning comes, I might not be putting them on again." I knew what she meant. As her son, it hurt to hear her say that. My mind would race with ideas of what my world would be like without my mother. I had already lost my father, and I didn't want to lose her, too. It was too heavy a burden for me to imagine life without her.

"If I die tonight and do not wake in the morning, I want you to run to your sister's house. Do you hear me? I want you to go straight there. Your sister will take care of you," she would say in the still darkness. Those were always the last words I would hear before going to sleep every night. And that was how I spent my childhood. It was difficult and filled with fear. Even now, as I think of those days, I can still feel the pain.

Even though all of China was suffering, our village stood out as a place that was in a serious state of crisis. Such an unusually high number of people were starving to death there that the Chinese government didn't have any choice but to face reality and finally start to deal with it. The government enacted feeding programs that helped to distribute food among the families in our village.

Even though we now were no longer dying, we were still suffering from hunger and malnutrition. We had very little food and no salt. My mother cut off her hair and sold it in order to buy rice and salt for us. As a result, she became the laughingstock of the entire village. I saw how the people laughed at her and how much shame she bore in her efforts just to feed us, and I felt an overwhelming sense of guilt.

The relationship between a son and his mother is a very special one. With my father gone, I was the only man in the house. Naturally, I wanted to protect my mother and comfort her. When she endured the shame of public humiliation to feed my younger sister and me, I felt responsible for it and in that way carried her burden, too. Her tears were my tears, and her shame was my shame. I felt helpless and ashamed for letting her go through such pain.

Many years later, on October 2, 2005, as I was sitting in a prison cell, I was suddenly overcome by the memory of my mother and all that she had done for me. I needed an outlet to tell her how I felt. Since she was no longer with me, I wrote down the following poem in Chinese:

My Mother,
You left me on March 4, 2003, at 86 years old.
I cried beside the bed where you slept,
I looked at you and my heart ached.
Your memory plays in my mind like a film:
It was springtime in 1962,
The year our nation ached with trouble.
We had no salt in our cupboards,
Yet you never neglected the health of your children.

You bought what we needed
    with the locks of your own hair.
Finally, my food had taste, but my heart was bleeding.
Passersby turned around to look at you,
Some even mocked you
    by calling you the "hairless woman."
Mother, I never should have eaten that salt,
I never should have let you cut your hair.
Mother, now your children are living much better,
But you are gone.
I wish that I could have kept you around for these years,
So that you could have tasted of the salt
    that your son has bought.

Even though we were barely able to find food during those days, my mother fought to find a way for me to go to school. Since my father was gone, it seemed impossible for me to be able to get an education, but she found a way. It is not easy being a single parent, and it is even harder when you are facing a famine due to unconscionable government policies that are killing everyone around you.

Though we were barely able to find food, my mother fought to find a way for me to go to school.

My mother did all that she could to send me to school, and although I attended for a time, she eventually arrived at the conclusion that she could no longer find the money needed to do so. She could barely scrape up enough money for us to eat. I really did not want to drop out of school because I knew that if I had any chance at finding a better life, it would have to be through education. My mother had done all that she could, and now I would need to do something.

One day, I thought of a way to raise funds to pay for school. During those days, since food was scarce, people would eat almost any kind of animal. I decided to go out in the fields and find moles to sell to the local villagers as meat. I had calculated in my head that if I sold fifty moles, I could raise sufficient funds to cover tuition for an entire semester of school. I also developed a crafty way of catching the moles that was quite successful. I was able to keep this lucrative business up for the next four years. Thanks to the moles, I earned enough to pay for my schooling. This kept my mother from having the extra worry of trying to find a way to pay for my education. After four years, however, the moles started to disappear from the Chinese countryside. It seemed that even they were falling victim to China's famine. Without any more moles to catch and sell, I could no longer pay for school and was forced to drop out.

My having to drop out of school was not easy on any of us. I felt that my future was slipping away. I tried to think of another way to pay for my education, but I was out of ideas, and my mother also needed my help at home. As much as I wanted to improve the future for our family, I knew that tomorrow was not certain for any of us. Mere survival took priority over education.

In 2005, I saw some moles in a field and was reminded of those difficult days. Now, whenever I notice moles in the countryside, I feel like waving to them and apologizing for how brutally I had treated their kind. I told myself those many years later that even though I hadn't been able to complete my education, I had to make good use of the investment of money I had put into my schooling by diligently studying the Scriptures in order to save human souls.

2

Grandfather Sun

March 11, 1963, is a date that I will never forget as long as I live. On that day, one of my family's elders, Sun Wendang, came to visit us as usual and took me aside to teach me. He was respected by everyone in our village for his wisdom and prudence.

Traditionally, the elderly have been highly respected in our culture and are cherished for the wisdom that they have gained throughout their years of life experience. At that time in China, houses were usually positioned so that several generations of one family lived in homes next to each other, forming a square around an enclosed courtyard. The most honored house in the compound belonged to the grandparents and was situated at the head of the courtyard. The children and grandchildren were then responsible for taking care of them and honoring them. It was the job of the elders to share their wisdom with their children and grandchildren so that this legacy of wisdom would be passed on to succeeding generations.

Sun Wendang was actually the brother of my grandfather, but I called him "Grandfather Sun" nonetheless. On that day in March, Grandfather Sun had something special for me. He planted in me the most valuable seed of wisdom I could ever receive. When he came over to me and pulled me close, it was clear that he had something important to share.

"My grandson, you are twelve years old now, and there is something that you should know. You are now old enough to receive a small nugget of wisdom that is eternal. What I am about to tell you is of eternal value and concerns the condition of your soul."

Jesus was not Someone with whom I was familiar. He didn't live in my village, so I hadn't heard of His family before.

I always listened to Grandfather Sun when he spoke to me, but this time seemed different. There was a special tone in his voice and an earnest look on his face that stressed the importance of his words. I couldn't help but notice these things and sat attentively to listen to his every word. I leaned forward, anxious to hear more, but I was not a patient child. The words seemed to be coming too slowly for me, and I wanted to reach into his mouth and pull them out faster. I knew that he had something exciting to share, and I wanted to hear it as quickly as possible!

"There is a friend I want to tell you about whose name is Jesus. Jesus was a Man without sin. You see, you and I are full of sin and wrongdoing. Sin is what we do when we wrong others, wrong our country, or wrong ourselves. Above all, there is a God, and we have also wronged Him—this is our great sin."

Grandfather Sun was trying to convey to me the concepts of sin and eternal life in a very simple way for my young mind to grasp. Although I was listening intently, I did not completely understand everything.

"You don't know Jesus, but Jesus knows you. He loves you. Jesus does not have any sin, and He wants to take away the burden of your sin. He wants to give you eternal life. The only way you can receive eternal life is if you are washed clean of your sin."

Although I'd had some exposure to church when I was four years old, I wasn't familiar with all the concepts Grandfather Sun was telling me about. There had been a very simple church not far from my home, but at the time I had been too young to understand what was being taught— and I wouldn't have noticed whether or not the church had freedom to worship.

Jesus was not Someone with whom I was familiar. He didn't live in my village, so I hadn't heard of His family before. My grandfather continued telling me about this unfamiliar Man.

"Jesus wants you to live with Him forever. He died for you in order to wash away your sins. He was beaten and crucified on a wooden cross, but on the third day He rose from the grave. He continues to live and one day will return and take us to heaven to be with Him forever."

When Grandfather Sun had finished speaking to me, I gave my life to Jesus and became a Christian. It was a special time that my grandfather and I shared together. After we prayed, he reached over and grabbed a Bible and placed it in my lap. I myself had never seen a Bible before, but at that time they were not so rare. The Cultural Revolution was still on the horizon, so it was not yet illegal to own one.

Grandfather Sun explained that he wanted to give me the Bible. When I looked at it, I felt a sudden joy because it was a special blessing to have my own Bible. However, reading it was not an easy task. Many of the words were new to me, and I was not a great reader because I had not gone very far in formal education. If fact, I couldn't read the Bible without using a dictionary.

Grandfather Sun opened up the Bible to Isaiah chapter 53 and began reading to me verses 2 through 6, which described Jesus. But instead of reading it word for word, he replaced some of the words with my name, so that it read like this:

> He had no beauty that Zhang Rongliang should desire Him. He is despised and rejected by Zhang Rongliang, a man of sorrows and acquainted with grief. And Zhang Rongliang hid, as it were, his face from Him; He was despised, and Zhang Rongliang esteemed Him not. Surely He has borne Zhang Rongliang's griefs and carried his sorrows; yet Zhang Rongliang did esteem Him stricken,

smitten by God, and afflicted. But He was wounded for Zhang Rongliang's transgressions, He was bruised for Zhang Rongliang's iniquities; the chastisement for Zhang Rongliang's peace was upon Him, and by His stripes Zhang Rongliang was healed. Zhang Rongliang is like a sheep who has gone astray; Zhang Rongliang has turned to his own way; and the Lord has laid on Him the iniquity of Zhang Rongliang.

After hearing that, I couldn't help but weep over the guilt of my sin and the high price the Lord had paid to take it from me. From that day on, I decided to follow Christ. The way Grandfather Sun read that passage has stayed with me until this day, and I will never forget it.

My older sister was also a Christian. She attended church, and one time, she took me with her. As a young teen, it all seemed very mysterious to me because our culture didn't have much exposure to Christianity. The only thing that I really remember about that visit is everyone praying together. My sister leaned over and told me, "Zhang, you are supposed to close your eyes when we pray." I didn't understand why. I thought you were supposed to close your eyes because something very mysterious and scary was about to happen that you weren't supposed to watch. I didn't know that there was a time to close your eyes at the beginning of prayer and to open your eyes at the end, so I kept my eyes closed even after the prayer was over.

When I heard people say, "Amen," I didn't know what that meant. I just kept my eyes closed. Even when everyone had finished praying and it was time to go home, I kept my eyes shut. I held on to my sister's hand, and she led me out of the church without looking at me. Only as we were walking home did she realize that I still had my eyes closed.

"What are you doing? Why are your eyes closed?" she asked.

"You told me to close my eyes!"

"Yes, but that is during prayer. We are not praying anymore. You can open them now."

It occurred to me that maybe the scary and mysterious things happened only when people were praying at church. Again, in those days, I wasn't too familiar with the activities of the church, and I associated some of them with Chinese superstition.

I was still attending school at the time I became a Christian, and the most obvious and measurable change in me was in regard to my studies. My grades improved drastically, and I became a much better student. This puzzled my teachers. Even at that young age, I was able to see the change in myself, and I gave all the praise to the Lord.

We didn't have a deep faith but only simple ideas about Jesus, as well as a hunger to learn more.

From what I read and from what Grandfather Sun taught me, I became aware of the Bible's teachings. Eventually, my mother also gave her life to Christ, so both of us were new believers. Needless to say, we didn't have a deep faith but only simple ideas about Jesus, as well as a hunger to learn more. It was difficult for my mother because she had never been to school and didn't know how to read, so she was unable to read the Bible.

In the spring of 1963, soon after we had decided to follow Christ, the government started a program to supply shoes to the poor people in our county. Our family didn't have shoes, and my mother and I walked around barefoot. The government sent around trucks full of shoes and offered them to the people in our county—but only if the recipients would agree to reject Jesus Christ.

I had heard about the program, so when my mother came home with shoes for us, I immediately wanted to know from whom she had gotten them. My worst fears were confirmed when she told me that she had received them from the government in accordance with the program.

It is hard to explain the betrayal that I felt at that moment. The government did not ask people to deny religion in general but specifically targeted Christians and gave the shoes only to those who denied Christ.

I felt so hurt. Knowing that my mother had openly denied Jesus Christ wounded me deeply. I lashed out at her in anger. We didn't know much about the Bible, but we knew that we should openly acknowledge Jesus before men. I began to cry uncontrollably. Nothing could comfort me.

"Give them back!" I shouted. "Give them back, or I will not go back to school." This was the only way that I could really get her attention. My mother deeply wanted me to go to school, and it would hurt her if I dropped out so early.

Looking back on it now, I can see how difficult it must have been for her. She was raising children on her own and wanted so much to give us things that we needed. We needed shoes, and she felt that the government program was a legitimate way she could get them for us. I know that she must have waited for a long time and fought through the crowds to get those shoes. It must not have been an easy task, but again, at the time, I felt betrayed. I felt that my mother had forsaken Jesus and, in turn, had forsaken me, too. Those were not easy days for any of us, but the choices that we would have to make in the future were not going to be any easier.

My mother did not keep the shoes. She gave them back to the government.

We all continued to struggle with poverty. My mother was a survivor. She lived every day in hunger, and as I wrote earlier, she even gave up her own hair to provide for us. She was a barefoot peasant and fought on every day to find a way to feed herself and her children.

In 1963, my mother remarried, and we moved to another town called Guaihe to live with my new stepfather. It was a change for all of us. My mother's new husband did not have a job, so our financial situation didn't change much, but living in Guaihe did bring about other opportunities that had not been available to us before.

There were people throughout the village of Guaihe who kept free-range sheep, and the locals needed someone to look after them. Guaihe was surrounded by mountains, and our home was at the top of a mountain. It was the perfect place to look after sheep, and the people of the town chose me as one of the shepherds. The owners didn't have enough money to pay to me, so they paid me in sheep. Because we lived so high up the mountain, we never really had anyone try to steal the animals from us. But although human thieves were never a problem, a different kind of thief was. I always had to be on the lookout for wolves.

I got to know the sheep well because I lived with them and even slept with them. I had to become knowledgeable about the different kinds of grass and what the sheep liked and didn't like. Our home was elevated enough off the ground that livestock could live under our floor. So, I often led the sheep to our home and kept them in our house in that space.

I gave each of the sheep a name and got close to them. When I first started looking after them, I felt that they were all the same, but after spending time with the animals and getting to know them, I realized that they were just as diverse as people are. I learned their personalities and observed that they were each unique. Certain sheep were afraid and timid, while others were brave and forceful. A few of them were curious and liked to explore far away from the herd; others were more cautious and never left the group.

By caring for the sheep, I developed an emotional connection with them. I treated them when they were sick; I protected them from wolf attacks; I helped to keep them together so that they would not get lost. I also observed their fear and empathized with them when it was time to take them to slaughter. They really became like a second family to me.

Sometimes, I would even have to settle conflicts among the sheep. That was my first course in conflict management, which would later come in handy for me as a pastor. In fact, all the time that I spent shepherding during those years would prove to be invaluable to me when I served as a pastor and leader in China's underground house churches.

3

The Cultural Revolution

June 1966 was a hot month. By that time, the notorious Cultural Revolution had begun. When many people think of that era, they often imagine the frenzied fanaticism for Mao Zedong and the Red Guards marching in parades, but they don't realize that it was also the era of one of the most brutal civil wars of the twentieth century. In China today, not many people discuss this dark period of their nation's history, and most books that say anything about the death and tragedy caused by the Cultural Revolution are banned.

Mao Zedong started the Revolution to prevent any possible drift toward capitalism in the nation. He felt that the struggle between the classes hadn't completely ended in 1949 but had instead taken on new and insidious forms. Even after all the wealthy landowners had been eliminated, he thought that there were new classes of intellectuals who might have maintained residual "bourgeois" values. Through an intense propaganda campaign, China's youth were led to declare war on the "four olds," zealously combating (1) old culture, (2) old customs, (3) old habits, and (4) old ideas. Part of this quest for newness meant the eradication of all ancient religions—especially Christianity, because of its historical ties with the West.

During the Cultural Revolution, Christian churches were torn down, Bibles were gathered up and set ablaze, and preachers and other Christians of all walks of life were arrested and severely persecuted. It was a dark time for the Chinese church.

Grandfather Sun was not immune to this widespread persecution. He was targeted by our local community because he was a well-known Christian. Grandfather endured much suffering for the sake of the gospel. He perceived that a great storm of persecution was coming; therefore, one day, he arranged for a couple of men to come to where I was living and bring me back to see him. When I arrived with the men, he handed me his own personal Bible. There was a look of urgency in his eyes, and his voice was tense. I don't know how, but he knew that his days were few and that he would not live to see the end of the impending storm.

As he handed me the Bible, he said, "My boy, this book is a heavenly book. It is our treasure in this life. You must guard it well and always keep it with you. The Bible should be with you as long as you live. Consider it more precious than your own life."

With great solemnity, I took his beloved Bible in my hands. I promised him that I would take care of it and guard it with my life. It was a large black Bible that had seen many years of wear. Its pages were full of markings from the many times Grandfather Sun had read it and made notes on the passages that stood out to him. The Bible was written in traditional Chinese characters, rather than the simplified script we were taught in school; it had been purchased in 1933 from a local church that had been in the area.

I took the Bible home with me. Because we lived high up in the mountains, it was more peaceful there and under less government control than other areas. I successfully hid the Bible in my pillow, and I would pull it out every evening to read it to my mother and sister. I read God's precious Word aloud to them because they were unable to read it for themselves. Sometimes, I would read to them until midnight. During those hard times, the words of the Lord brought much comfort to our weary souls.

Not long after giving me his Bible, Grandfather Sun was publicly humiliated and tortured, receiving a martyr's crown in the end. He was brought out by local officials and forced to walk down our hometown street with a board hanging around his neck on which was written in huge letters, "Follower of Jesus." Oh, what a glorious thing to be called! He was marked as an antirevolutionary and humiliated by the Communist Party.

As a young man, I watched this happen; how painful it was for me to see him marched through the streets while being taunted and abused by vicious townspeople.

Grandfather Sun was forced to wear a tall hat, made out of newspaper, that resembled a Western dunce cap. He looked like a helpless lamb among wolves, but unlike the sheep that I cared for, he couldn't look to me for protection. My helplessness in the situation brought me great sorrow.

Before he died, Grandfather Sun looked at me and said, "Continue to preach the good news of Jesus Christ, whether the time is right or not."

Before he died, Grandfather Sun looked at me and said, "My boy, I believe the Lord will greatly use you for His purpose. I am going home now. Remember this with all your might: Continue to preach the good news of Jesus Christ, whether the time is right or not." (See 2 Timothy 4:2.) Those words stay with me even now. They linger in my memory and have been stamped on my mind as the true mark of sacrifice: "...whether the time is right or not."

1967 marked the second year of the Revolution. Christians were scattered everywhere as the persecution increased. We were all in full retreat. All church doors had been shut, and no one was holding open meetings or Bible studies. We were on the doorstep of the darkest years in our history.

After reading in the book of Hebrews, *Let us not give up the habit of meeting together, as some are doing* (Hebrews 10:25 GNT), I realized that it was not right for us to stop coming together as believers. The Bible didn't say, "Let us not give up the habit of meeting together...unless it gets too difficult and the persecution becomes too great." This was clearly not the teaching of Scripture.

I decided that we needed to continue meeting together in fellowship, regardless of the cost. We began to come together in secret underground meetings. At first, there were only three to five of us. Since I had a Bible and had been studying the Word of God, I naturally became the leader of the meetings.

When we came together, we would pray and sing songs quietly so that others could not hear us. In the beginning, it was just my sister, my mother, a couple of neighbors, and me. I would read simple stories from the Bible and would share very simple ideas and messages drawn from them.

After my mother and I discussed the situation, we decided that it would be good to have regular meetings in our home. Since doing so was very dangerous, many people advised us, "You must be as wise as serpents but as harmless as doves." (See Matthew 10:16.) They didn't understand why we would want to bring unnecessary trouble upon ourselves during such a perilous time. It didn't make sense to many of the brothers and sisters in our community.

When we started having illegal church meetings in our home, most of our neighbors were too afraid to attend, even though they wanted to. Although everyone else was too frightened to join us, my mother and I decided that the two of us would share the Word of the Lord and sing His praises in our home. With just the two of us there, it really felt as if we were having the smallest church service in the history of the world. But we knew that the Lord was with us no matter how small our meetings were because He promised that He would always be with His people.

After we'd been holding home meetings for six months, others began to attend, as well. At that point, about five people were coming. By the following year, in 1968, attendance had increased to thirteen. We didn't have much, but we all had the same mind, loved one another, and participated in the meeting.

In those days, we didn't have anyone who could teach us, and we didn't have a radio by which we could hear Christian programming. Neither did we have inspirational books or commentaries. All we had were the words of Scripture. We prayed that the Lord would help us to understand what we were reading. The Scriptures spoke directly to us and would move us to tears. We would hold hands and cry with one another as we prayed together. We cried out to God, and He responded. Our services often carried on for hours because no one wanted to stop worshipping or go home.

We also saw miracles take place, such as the healing of the sick. I remember that my uncle had become really ill and was dying. We prayed for him and shared with him about the saving power of Jesus. He had idols in his home, so we went there and destroyed all of them. Two days later, he woke up from a state of unconsciousness and called out for food. He was completely healed and hungry!

My uncle's father was not able to read Chinese characters. We prayed for him, believing that Jesus could enable him to read. After our prayer, he immediately received the ability to read Chinese!

Word began to get around about the unique church meetings in our home, and more and more people began to attend. Soon there were too many of us, so we had to divide into two groups. We looked for another home that would be safe to have church services in and decided to start another meeting in Guangquan, a town not far from us. In the midst of China's darkest hour, God was with us and was multiplying His church.

4

The Er Qi Community Gang

On July 28, 1967, my mother came to me while I was tending sheep in the mountains and asked me to leave the flock and go into town to buy some basic items like salt, matches, and lamp oil. When I arrived in town, two gangs were battling each other in the streets. At that time in Henan, there were two main gangs—one called "Henan Rebellion Head" and the other "Er Qi Community." Both groups were Communist revolutionaries, but they were fiercely opposed to one another, and they would fight deadly pitched battles in the streets.

Since each gang was comprised of local workers' union members, most people in the town were there fighting that day and protesting in the streets instead of working. It was utter chaos. Finally, Er Qi Community was defeated.

I had tried to keep a safe distance from the conflict but watched as the events unfolded right in front of me. When I returned to my village, I told the neighbors about the battle I had seen. Mao Zedong had just come to Zhengzhou, the capital of Henan Province, and had voiced his approval of Er Qi Community. However, due to how slowly news traveled during those days, the two rebel groups were not aware that Mao had just endorsed one group over the other.

Because I had returned to my village and told everyone what had happened, all the villagers assumed that I had participated in the conflict. Word began to spread that I was a part of the rebellion. That false rumor quickly earned me a name in the village, along with new friends—and new enemies.

After I had shared with others what I had just witnessed of the battle and had given the items I had purchased to my mother, I went back to the pastures to tend my sheep. I didn't know that the Henan Rebellion leadership had begun looking for me. They thought that I was fighting against them and wrongly assumed that I was a leader in the opposing rebel gang. I was outside with my sheep when representatives from both rebel groups arrived at my home.

My mother had had a dream the night before in which I was a small donkey and several people needed me to help them by carrying out tasks. When the leaders of the two gangs arrived at my home, my mother brought them to me. The leader of Er Qi Community assumed that I was on his side and asked me to join his gang. The other rebellion gang leader had come with the intention of making me march through the street with a sign around my neck in order to shame me in front of everyone.

The leader of Er Qi Community said, "We have been through this village, and it appears that you are the only one here who approves of our movement. We are certain that we will win and would like you to join us and become the leader for this area."

"But I am not a part of any rebellion," I told him. "I am just a farmer tending my sheep. I have not taken any side in this conflict."

I wanted to stay out of the fight, but at the same time, the offer seemed exciting to me. To join the rebellion was an honorable thing during those days in China. It would be a way to honor my country and make my family proud. It didn't occur to me at the time that the Communist Party was opposed to my faith. I thought of it only in terms of patriotism for my country. I was proud to be Chinese and wanted to serve China to the best of my ability.

I made the choice to join hands with the Er Qi Community gang. I thought that by merely joining the rebellion movement supported by Mao Zedong and the Communist Party, I was writing myself a ticket to a more prosperous future. All of my neighbors told me how lucky I was that I had the opportunity to join the rebellion movement. At the time, to my mind, it was an example of all things working together for the good of those who love the Lord. (See Romans 8:28.)

I was excited about the New China, and I fully supported the ideas of the revolution. I read Mao Zedong's "Little Red Book," which we were forced to own, read, and carry with us at all times. I was motivated to do these things and to enforce the book's teachings. I memorized it entirely and could recite it upon request. Like a good revolutionary, I studied it diligently and carried it with me everywhere I went.

I was excited about the New China, and I fully supported the ideas of the revolution.

What can I say? I was young and full of the often-misguided enthusiasm of youth. There was a fever sweeping the nation under Mao Zedong, and it was being ushered in by young patriots like me. All of the rules and traditions of old China were being removed from society. Women were being liberated from the days of being uneducated and having their feet bound (a torturous practice in which little girls had their feet wrapped tightly with cloth to prevent their feet from growing as they matured to adulthood). All of the foolish superstitions related to ancestor worship were also being cast off. Taoist and Buddhist temples were being smashed to rubble, along with their idols. Imperialist foreign occupiers were being thrown out of the country in droves; and the oppressive class system, with its idea of hereditary royalty, was no longer being practiced.

Every person was considered equal and would be given equal pay for his work. Doctors would no longer make more money than the hardworking trash collector. The landowner would no longer hold power over the peasant who was forced to rent land in order to feed his family. The factory owner could no longer work his employees day and night like slaves. Everyone was expected to work according to his abilities and get paid according to his needs. It was a wonderful time of liberation and equality, and we were young and eager to seize the moment.

I quickly excelled in the Communist Party as a member of Er Qi Community. I was put in charge of the administration for my entire area. I helped train young people, and I enforced laws that broke off old cultural traditions. I even carried a gun when I was sent out to arrest those deemed antirevolutionary. It felt to me like China's golden age had finally come, and I was playing a key part in it.

There were many small things that were no longer allowed in the New China. For instance, women were not allowed to wear jewelry or high heels. During a wedding ceremony, people were no longer permitted to give dresses or special clothes to the bride but were allowed to give only practical gifts that would help the bride and groom work in the field, such as shovels or work gloves—anything that could be used for labor.

I wore a red band on my arm, which gave me access to a lot of benefits. I was able to eat for free and travel on the train without cost. I was the top supervisor for my area, and I was given an office to carry out my duties. I was placed in charge of thirty-six villages and had more than 1,170 people working for me. I prayed to God and thanked Him for the opportunity to serve Him at such a high level. I promised to use my power and authority to help advance His church in my area.

I wanted to use my power and political influence to keep Christians from being humiliated as Grandfather Sun had been. I was able to keep Bibles from being confiscated and destroyed. With so many people under my command, I felt that I had a considerable amount of influence and could really make a difference. I was making an impact on my community for the good of my country, and I wanted to continue doing so to the best of my ability.

As far as my faith was concerned, even though I had been saved and was holding secret Bible studies in our home, there was still one thing I hadn't done yet—I had never been baptized.

When I first became a Christian while sitting beside Grandfather Sun, I didn't know anything about being a Christian, and the need to be baptized had never occurred to me. When I was older and had learned more, it was not a safe situation in China, and I wasn't able to be baptized. It wasn't until the freezing winter of 1968 that I decided to undergo baptism.

Even today, many Chinese in our church wait to be baptized in the winter because it is considered by many to be the best time for it. In China, we believe that baptism is a unique outward sign of an inward change. The opinion of many Chinese Christians is that being baptized in the summer is very much like bathing. In a culture where many people often bathe in rivers and lakes, there doesn't seem to be anything special about being immersed in water outdoors. "People go to the river to bathe during the summer months all the time," they say. "How can that be special?" Thus, being baptized in cold water during the winter is considered to be a stronger sign of death, sacrifice, and true commitment to the Christian faith.

I was to be baptized by a local believer along with thirty other people. It was against the law to take part in such a ceremony, but it was something that I considered to be important. We all came together shortly before midnight and walked quietly along a small path in the dark toward a pond in the middle of the forest. Among the group was a fellow brother who was a dear servant of God involved in full-time ministry who was visiting the area at the time. He was a preacher who lived a godly life.

We arrived at the pond and waited until after midnight, keeping watch to make sure no one else could see us. Although there were more than thirty of us altogether, I was the only one who supported the Communists; I was even wearing the red band around my arm at the time.

> It was against the law to take part in a baptism ceremony, but it was something that I considered to be important.

It was an exciting moment. I could feel my heart race as I thought about the honor of being baptized. Often, baptisms in China are not ceremonies that only friends and family come together to witness. People are frequently baptized with other Christians to whom they are not related; they might not even know these fellow believers outside of underground church meetings.

In those early days, we didn't know much about baptism, but we witnessed many miracles take place during them. That night, a believer who had a life-threatening fever wanted to be baptized. Some brothers and sisters tried to convince him that it would not be wise to trek out to the wilderness in the winter and be submerged in icy water, but their pleas fell on deaf ears. He was determined to obey his Lord in baptism. When he was baptized, he emerged from the water without any fever, completely healed of his illness.

Such things were not uncommon in those days. Another believer whom I knew had been given only a short time to live wanted to be baptized before he died; but following the baptism, he was completely healed of the terminal illness.

After I was baptized, I became even more excited about sharing the gospel of Jesus Christ. I started to travel to other areas to preach about Jesus. First, I went back to my birthplace. I sought out my close relatives and friends, and I preached to them about salvation through our Lord and Savior. Within a short time, four of my relatives came to the Lord and were saved. The following year, I traveled to Nanzhao and successfully led five more souls to Christ.

At that time, everything I put effort into seemed to succeed. I believed that the favor of the Lord was with me and that He had blessed my going forth and my coming in. (See Psalm 121:8.) I was seeing the church grow more and more. Even in my personal life serving the Party, I could see the hand of the Lord moving in miraculous ways.

5

"I Stand with Jesus Christ"

On July 1, 1970, I was accepted into the Chinese Communist Party. This was considered to be a great honor because, despite there being only one political party in China that everyone had to support, not everyone could be a member of it. Even though I had faithfully carried out the laws and orders of the Party, up to that point I had not been allowed to join. I considered myself a pioneer for the Communist Party and wanted to bring revolution to my country. I was determined to see everyone treated equally, the rich paying their fair share and the poor being lifted up.

Because of the loyalty I had shown in my duties and the determination that I had displayed in serving the Party, a few fellow cadre members invited me to join. All my comrades were impressed with my support of Mao Zedong, and word about my work went up through the chain of command.

I was interviewed by several senior cadre members from other areas. They tested me, asking various questions about my knowledge of the Party, my commitment to Mao, and my dedication to the revolution. During the evaluation process, I was asked several times if I believed in a myth or a superstition. Many Chinese Christians had a problem with this question because they felt it referred to religion, and thus not many believers joined the Communist Party. However, since I had never considered my relationship with Christ to be associated with either a myth or a superstition, I had no problem telling them that I didn't believe in such things. I didn't imagine that there might be a conflict between my being a Christian and my taking a verbal oath to serve the Communist Party until death.

After an intense evaluation period, I was marched out with about one thousand others to the main plaza in the center of the town of Guaihe. That day, we joined the Communist Party in a special ceremony. Each of us was given a certificate, and I hoped mine would be my ticket out of poverty. I was very excited.

I didn't imagine that there might be a conflict between my being a Christian and my taking a verbal oath to serve the Communist Party.

I was placed at the top of the chain of command for my area. There was technically one person above me, but I didn't have to answer to him, and I made all of the command decisions in my area of responsibility. To have been given this position at such a young age was a huge honor. It was clear that the hand of the Lord was at work, because I was not as well-educated as the others and did not have any family connections to the Party as the other comrades had.

Because of the huge honor bestowed upon me, I decided to work even harder to serve my country and to root out antirevolutionaries in China with even more fervor than previously. I was only nineteen years old, but I didn't want to waste one minute. I had a huge responsibility, and I wanted to show everyone that I was able to carry out my duties in a responsible and efficient manner for the Party and for the nation.

Mao's Little Red Book went with me everywhere I went. I had memorized his words so that they were burned into my heart. I also read the Scriptures every chance I got. During the day, I was serving the Party; in the evening, I was serving the Lord. To be honest, I never thought of serving the Party as anything separate from serving the Lord. In my heart, I still believe that every good follower of Jesus Christ is by default a good citizen. As Christians, we are to abide by the law, help the poor, bring justice to the weak, pray for our leaders, and give to the community. As a follower of Jesus, my faith had been evident when I had excelled at school and hadn't been a troublemaker. My faith was also evident when I worked hard and excelled at my job. The Communist Party seemed to mimic the goals of my faith by helping the helpless, feeding the poor, and bringing equality to all men and women.

Things began to change for me on the evening of May 22, 1971. The local Party committee clerk, Jinde Li, came to me and said, "I have good news, Zhang. Because of the great work that you have been doing, coupled with the fact that you are trustworthy and loyal, a request has been made to make you a government official on the national level, not just on the local level. You have one week to go and share the good news with your family and comrades and to pass your current duties over to someone else. Return to me in six days, and I will immediately begin the process of plugging you into your new position." He paused for a minute, then said, "You are only twenty years old, Zhang. I hope you have the ability to grasp the concept of what a golden opportunity this is for you."

The news was shocking. I sat and soaked it all in, trying to imagine what it was going to be like to move up to the national level of the Communist Party. I tried to envision what I would be doing and where I would be living. I was asked to attend a ceremony that evening marking the new promotion. I have to admit, I was also enticed at the idea of more power and more money. The new position they offered would allow me to have a better life. No one in my family had ever had such an opportunity. We had been peasants for many generations, and this was a once-in-a-lifetime chance to change everything—for not only myself, but also for future generations. However, the same day, I received a secret note from a church leader in our area inviting me to a baptism meeting that night. It would have been understandable for me not to attend the baptism and to go to the Party ceremony, instead. I think that most people would have understood, but, for some reason, I felt in my heart that I was supposed to be at this baptism meeting.

I had finally reached a fork in the road; the two options were heading in different directions. I was torn between being faithful to the Party and being faithful to the church. I knelt down before the Lord and began to pray. Soon after I started praying, I felt something inside of me say, *Honor*

Jesus as number one. It became clear that I needed to skip the Party meeting and attend the baptism service.

I didn't know it then, but that decision would change my life forever. We were at the height of the Cultural Revolution, and holding secret meetings in the middle of the night was considered an act of high treason. (Mao Zedong had employed clandestine meetings to bring about his revolution and rise to power; he had hosted private meetings with labor unions and university students in preparation for staging the overthrow of the Nationalists. He knew how easily secret meetings could lead to conspiracies and coups, so one of the first things he did as chairman was to make it illegal to congregate in secret.)

Without warning, the soldiers kicked in the door and immediately encircled us, pointing rifles at our faces.

The church leader who had arranged the baptism service was a dear brother named Yao Wanming. About one hundred sixty people came together that night. Our church had been growing over the previous several months, and there was a great need for baptisms. We were never able to keep up with the baptisms because of the limitations of having to do everything in secret. I was assigned the task of filling out the forms for everyone who was about to be baptized.

Before we started the baptisms, Yao Wanming preached a message to everyone in attendance. Everything was going smoothly, and we were about to go out to the pond where the actual baptisms would take place. During those days, we would often take off our shoes and walk with them under our arms to keep from making too much noise outside. This time, however, no one would make it out the door.

Unknown to us, more than thirty soldiers had surrounded the house. Without warning, they kicked in the door and immediately encircled us, pointing rifles at our faces. There was nowhere to run, and most of us didn't even have our shoes on.

I looked up and saw the faces of young men who worked for me. I was actually their commander and could easily have started barking orders, but at that moment, I knew that I wasn't in any position to tell anyone to do anything. I had been caught doing something that was completely illegal in the eyes of the Party.

The room was not very well lit, so no one recognized me. Even though I knew who they were, they did not know who I was. None of my comrades in the raid that night would ever have guessed that I was one of the participants in the illegal meeting. I had never been in trouble with the law before, so this was the first time I would be arrested. In the fog of my shock and confusion, the time went by very fast. It was as if time was standing still but somehow simultaneously moving quickly.

Suddenly, two soldiers grabbed one of the brothers, Gao Daoxue, who was praying. The soldiers began to beat him and kick him on the ground. They were swift and violent, showing no mercy. Brother Gao yelled out the name of Jesus and continued to pray while enduring the fierce blows.

One of the soldiers pointed at the rest of us and said, "If you are willing to deny the name of Jesus and throw away your nonsense, we will let you go home tonight. You will not be arrested. If you do not deny this superstition, then a living hell full of hard labor is waiting for you tomorrow. You will be digging sand and repairing roads, and we will march you out in the streets so that everyone will know what kind of antirevolutionary scum you are."

There was a moment of silence as they waited for our response. The soldier peered over his rifle and looked at us with disdain and disgust. I knew what he was thinking because, in many ways, I was like him. I, too, was zealous to protect our country and committed to support the revolution. I, too, wanted to root out the antirevolutionaries.

As he waited for a response, a brother next to me began to loudly sing, "Get up! Let's go! Leave all behind and take up your cross to follow the Lord to Calvary."

As he shouted out the song, the other believers in the room looked up to heaven and began to sing without fear, as well. Tears began to flow down our faces as we sang the song with conviction. That song took on new meaning as we faced the soldiers who wanted to harm us. The power of the Lord came upon us, and we felt comforted by His presence. As we sang, I could sense that the soldiers had been taken a little off guard and were perhaps even convicted by the words of the song.

All of us were arrested and taken to city hall to be processed the following day. As we arrived at city hall, the guards kept us under their watch. None of us was able to sleep that night, because we didn't know what would happen. There weren't any beds in city hall, anyway. I was anxious for the morning to come so that I could immediately begin contacting my coworkers.

Because of the darkness of night, my identity was still unknown. When dawn began to break, I walked up to one of the soldiers and told him that I needed to meet with Mr. Ai, who was the county clerk. I was taken to him and noted the shocked expression on his face when I walked into his office.

"Zhang, what are you doing here?"

I explained the situation. He listened intently as I told him everything that had happened.

"Why didn't you let me know earlier?" he responded. "I am so sorry that you were left outside to suffer last night. If I had only known that you were in the group that was arrested, I would have done something."

Ai took me to meet with another clerk, Li Jinde, who was higher up the chain of command. When I met with Li, I recounted to him everything that had taken place the night before.

"Comrade Li, last night I attended a meeting in a home that is owned by a friend. It was a meeting of Christians who had come together to practice our faith. We were arrested last night and brought to city hall to spend the night. I have waited until now to come and share this with you so that you can deal with it."

"Zhang," he said as he looked me in the eye, "you are a young man. Don't be so hard on yourself. It is normal for all of us to make mistakes.

What is most important is that you don't make the same mistake again in the future. It is not as big of a problem as you think. This is what I want you to do. Leave here, go back home, write a confession of your crime, and bring the letter back to me."

I departed from Li's office and began to think about what I would write. As I put pen to paper, I began to tell the story of my life and my conversion. I wrote about why I had given my life to Christ and the details of Grandfather Sun's influence on me. I wrote about all the changes that had happened to me in my life, and I ended the letter with the promise of Jesus' return to earth to take us all home to be with Him.

I returned to Li's office and handed him my letter. He received it and began to read. As he continued reading, his facial expression changed from one of going through a procedure to one of confusion. He said, "Well, you are not sorry at all for what you have done! This is not a confession letter. Are…are you trying to convert me? This is completely unacceptable, Zhang. You know that this is unacceptable.

"You have only one choice here, and the choice *should* be clear," he continued. "You are a member of the Communist Party. We are atheists. You cannot be a Christian, Zhang, and be a member of the Communist Party. You have to choose one or the other. You cannot be both. It would be a disaster if you chose not to deny Jesus."

He thought for a moment about how to handle the situation.

"Let's do this. What I would like for you to do is to go home tonight and think about what you are doing. I want you to write this letter again and hand it to me in the morning."

I nodded.

> I had a clear choice between happiness or suffering, the Party or Jesus, freedom or prison, the world or heaven— eternal death or eternal life.

"Remember, Zhang, this is your last chance. You will not get another one. This is important. This might be the most important letter of your life, so take it seriously. What you write in that letter will decide your destiny."

That night, as I sat down to write the letter again, I knew that what I wrote had the power to determine my future. I just needed to decide what kind of future I wanted to have. I had a clear choice between happiness or suffering, the Party or Jesus, freedom or prison, the world or heaven—eternal death or eternal life.

I couldn't eat or sleep. I knelt down before the Lord and began to pray. After a short time of prayer, I stood up, determined to write what I must. What was I debating? I had already decided to follow Jesus and had no intention of turning back. I wanted to keep my position in the Party, but I could not turn my back on my Lord and Savior.

As I began to pray again, I felt Jesus standing by my side, and suddenly a couple of Scripture verses came to me. God laid these words from the Song of Solomon on my heart: *"Love is as powerful as death; passion is as strong as death itself. It bursts into flame and burns like a raging fire. Water cannot put it out; no flood can drown it. But if any tried to buy love with their wealth, contempt is all they would get"* (Song of Solomon 8:6–7 GNT).

In that moment, I was empowered to make my decision. I said, "Jesus, You are all that matters to me. You matter most in this life. How can I do anything other than chose You?"

The following morning, I handed in my note. I ended it with, "I stand with Jesus Christ—how great is the salvation that He has brought; nothing can compare to it."

There were several people in the head office when I handed in my letter. One of the officials who took it from me read it and became angry. "This is what you are giving me?" he growled.

"Absolutely," I said confidently.

"You are gambling with your life here. Are you sure you won't regret it?"

"I am sure," I replied.

    With that, I was dismissed. As I turned and walked out of the office, I felt a fresh sweetness flooding over me that is hard to explain. There is a special joy in knowing that you have done the right thing, even when you know that it will lead to a future of hardship.

6

Interrogation, Torture, and Labor Camp

On June 2, 1971, I was ordered to present myself at the local police station. I was detained there while a small detachment was sent to my home to look for my Bible and any other religious writings that might be there. I knew that they would not find my Bible. I often lent it to others, and we had a system of shuffling it around from one house to another to keep it from being discovered by the police. When I had it at home, I would often take it up into the mountains and hide it under a rock, but that ended up not being a very good hiding place because the Bible would frequently get wet and be damaged.

The team tore apart my home piece by piece while I sat at the police station. They knew that I had a Bible, but I would not tell them where it was, and they couldn't find it. In the end, they found only a hymnal, but you would have thought they had found a thousand Bibles. They were so happy with the hymnal, believing that they had found a sacred treasure.

Once they had the hymnal, they immediately recommended that I be prosecuted in front of the judge for owning an illegal book. Even though I knew that a hymnal was not the same as a Bible, to the Party officials, it was just as incriminating.

Shortly before I was caught at the baptism service, an older Christian of retirement age had been singing songs of praise by himself. A Party official had heard him and asked what he was singing about. When the old gentleman explained it to him, the official asked, "Do you hate socialism?

Hasn't the Communist Party treated you well? Are you trying to engage in class warfare?" The man was reported to the authorities and eventually sentenced to four years in a reeducation camp.

If he got four years for singing a song, they might want the death penalty for me since they found an entire hymnal, I thought to myself.

When the search party returned to the jail, they had my hymnal in their hands. They waved it around and showed the others their prized treasure.

"Where did you get this?" they demanded as they looked at me. "Who gave you this song book?"

"No one gave it to me. I wrote the songs in that book."

The things that I had taught others to do against antirevolutionaries were about to be used against me.

"I don't think so. You couldn't have written the songs in this book. You are too stupid. You didn't even finish school. You can barely read, let alone write songs!"

Their questions became more and more intense, and I slowly began to realize that I would not be going home. The tables had turned. No longer would I be the one interrogating but rather the one being interrogated. The things that I had taught others to do against antirevolutionaries were about to be used against me, and I was not anxious to find out how well I had taught them.

I was sent to a private cell where they continued to question me, saying, "Where did you get that book? Who gave it to you? Who is distributing illegal contraband?"

I didn't answer, but I was getting hungry because they had stopped feeding me. They were deliberately depriving me of food so that I would be more apt to break. First food deprivation, then sleep deprivation. I knew the cycle, but this was my first time on the other side of the questioning table. I knew how things were going to be, but it didn't make them any easier.

Communism does something very evil to a person. It takes away the personalization of individuals. In fact, any social institution that systematically removes belief in God does this. We Christians understand that we are all brothers and sisters in Christ Jesus. We are a family. We even recognize that nonbelievers are created in the image of God. There is also the Golden Rule, which says, *Do to others as you would have them do to you*" (Luke 6:31 NIV). When we are in Christ Jesus, it is not possible for us to torture others, because true Christians are conscious of a reversal of roles. It is impossible for a Christian to look into the eyes of a victim being tortured and not empathize with that person, even to the point of flinching with each blow.

Atheism takes that shared commonality away. Communism in China during those days dehumanized society. In accordance with evolutionary theories, people were devalued to the level of animals. People were no longer people; they were expendable. They were not thought of as sons and daughters, mothers and fathers, and brothers and sisters but as a collective, machinelike workforce that needed to produce more than it consumed.

It was not easy for me to sit in that cell and think about the high position I used to have and how I had served the Party with everything that was in me. It was then that I began to be convicted about my pursuit of Communism. Slowly, I would abandon all of my erroneous and naïve ideas about the Party.

The words of Mao Zedong no longer brought me the comfort they had in the past. I would never again find enthusiasm in his Little Red Book; instead, all of my strength and joy would be found in the Scriptures of my Lord, whom I knew would never leave me or forsake me. (See, for example, Hebrews 13:5.)

I was interrogated every day. I kept on getting weaker from lack of food. The guards would punch me to the ground and then kick me. Every blow seemed to jolt my entire body more and more as I weakened from hunger. They were losing patience, and I was losing consciousness.

On the third day, my frail body was exhausted and depleted of sustenance. The summer heat was inescapable. There was no bed, and it was hard for me to sleep on the floor. I tried to find the coolest place on the floor on which to lie in order to keep from sweating. I knew that the more

I sweated, the more dehydrated I would become, but eventually I was too weak to care.

At night, two guards would watch over me, and we all knew each other. They asked, "Why are you doing this, Zhang? Why can't you just give up your foolish beliefs and work with us?"

What could I say? How could I help them understand that the love of Jesus is greater than any love we might experience in this world? How could they possibly comprehend that truth when all they could see was a stubborn fool enduring unnecessary torture?

> **How could they possibly comprehend the love of Jesus when all they could see was a stubborn fool enduring unnecessary torture?**

The guards who interrogated me were actually friends of mine. I eventually told them that the book had come from a man by the name of Sun Wendang. They were happy that I had finally given them some useful information. After I gave them the name, they left the room and allowed me to bathe and eat some food.

Not long afterward, the guards came bursting back into the room in a rage. One of them immediately smacked me in the face and said, "You lied to us! Sun Wendang is already dead."

"I didn't lie to you. He wrote the songs, but that was three years ago. You wanted a name, and I gave you a name."

There were exasperated with me. "Why do you have to be so stubborn, Zhang? Just tell us where you got the stupid book! You have only one choice. You cannot serve the Party and believe in Jesus. You could have been successful, but instead you chose to be a Christian. Now you must suffer the consequences."

While I was still at the police station, the local government sent another group of officers to my hometown to look for other antirevolutionary

Christians. They soon learned that there were at least ten people in my village who also believed in Jesus. The police threatened them in order to get additional information on other believers. Those ten believers were detained and beaten until they gave information about other believers and meetings in the village.

Unexpectedly, one man began to talk. He told the police that I did indeed have a Bible, but I kept it hidden. This was what the police had suspected. They knew that there was more than just a hymn book at my house. They wanted that Bible.

I didn't want to be tortured anymore, but I knew that if I lost that Bible, I might never get another one. I thought of dear Grandfather Sun who had given it to me and of the words that he had shared with me before he was martyred. In essence, he had said, "Zhang, you must live and die with that Bible. No matter what, you must not allow them to get it." That Bible was my life. It was a family treasure, and I knew I had to guard it and keep it safe.

Although I didn't know it at the time, there was a fellow believer from our church in the courtyard right outside the jail. He was pretending to be a street sweeper and was walking around sweeping dirt. He was sweeping all around the courtyard area, all the while peeking into windows and open doors to see if he could get a glimpse of me. After some time, we saw each other.

When I had a few minutes alone without the guards watching, he came over, and I whispered to him to hurry to my home and see my mother. "You have to find a way to meet my mother and get her this message," I said with urgency. "Tell her to find two random books and burn them in the yard. Tell her not to clean up the mess after she burns them but to leave the ashes there in the yard."

I looked around to see if anyone was looking or listening in on our conversation. I knew that we didn't have much time. "Tell her that when the police return to look for the Bible again, to tell them that it was already destroyed, and to take them to the place where she burned the other books and show them the ashes."

My friend nodded in acknowledgment and left. When the police returned to my home, my mother had already burned the books as I had asked her to. She took the police out to the yard and pointed to the remaining ashes. After inspecting the burned books, they concluded that they must have been Bibles.

They thought they had finally destroyed my Bible, but they were still not satisfied because they had not destroyed my faith. I had been at the police station for twenty-nine days, and the days were not getting easier.

Then the police had an idea they thought might break me down and bring me to my senses. Since sitting in a room and being tortured was not working, they proposed sending me to a labor camp for three days. Perhaps forcing me to work outside without stopping for three days would do the trick. The police led me out of the jail and took me to a labor camp that was about ten miles from my home. I was not allowed to see my family or any members of our church.

They thought they had finally destroyed my Bible, but they were still not satisfied because they had not destroyed my faith.

A three-day sentence at the labor camp somehow turned into one year. For an entire year, I was forced to labor under the watchful eyes of the prison guards. The things I experienced in that camp were far worse than what I had endured at the police station. During my entire time at the camp, I was forbidden to talk to other people—a punishment that was incredibly hard for me to endure.

One of the worst punishments for a pastor is to be prohibited from speaking to others. Working with people, preaching the gospel, and sharing in the lives of others are some of the passions God has given me. It was pure torture not to be able to talk to anyone.

One day, a young man by the name of Li who was also imprisoned at the camp came to see me, but it was not possible for me to speak with him. I wanted to share with him so much that I feared my words would start coming out of the pores of my skin if I didn't open my mouth. Li was a well-educated man who was full of passion and love for the Lord. I prayed in my heart for God to help me find a way to speak with him.

Soon after my prayer, the Lord gave me the idea that we could go into the bathroom to speak together. Next to the toilets, we were able to share with one another. It was for only about two minutes at a time, but those brief moments were incredibly filling. They were exactly what I needed. Li encouraged me, and I encouraged him; we had a camaraderie that connected us immediately. Indeed, the bond of Christ is stronger than any other.

Soon, we realized that the bathroom was actually a great place for us to meet. We would go in at different times and spend a few minutes sharing and encouraging one another. After realizing that I was able to meet with brother Li, I arranged to meet others in the bathroom, as well.

In our own humble way, we were holding church services over the filthy holes in the ground that were the camp's crude toilets. The smells that wafted up from below were not enjoyable in the least, but the fellowship was a sweet aroma to our souls. I am convinced that we can have church services anywhere if our hearts are truly close to the Lord.

It is essential for the members of Christ's body to edify and lift each other up. Making yourself vulnerable to your brother in need is absolutely necessary so that both of you can be broken before the Lord and rely on His sustaining power to pull you through hard times. During my first imprisonment, I knew that I could not endure the suffering by myself. There was no way I could have survived without the power of the Lord to uphold me, and He did so by bringing brothers to my side during that dark time.

Those brothers were not men with whom I would have had anything in common outside the prison walls. They had formerly been hardened criminals, and at first, many of them were cold and shut off to the emotions of others. However, once they had accepted the Lord Jesus Christ into their hearts, they became my lifelong friends and partners in ministry. I thank the Lord for each one of those precious souls.

7

The Black Five

After a year of imprisonment, I had begun to settle into a daily routine. I meditated on God's goodness during the day, as it was the only thing that could sustain me. I also woke up to pray three times every night. I depended on the strength that God alone could provide.

My time in prison got only more difficult over the next couple of years. I was forced to work in an intensive labor team assembled with the express purpose of working people to death. The government had decided that I would be forced to work with the "Black Five."

The term "Black Five" was used to describe the enemies of Mao Zedong's socialist society. Class warfare was in full swing at that time. The zealous youth movement in the Communist Party had declared certain members of society as class enemies. "The Black Five," or "Five Black Categories," were in opposition to the "Five Red Categories."

The Five Red Categories consisted of the revolutionary cadres, martyrs, soldiers, workers, and poor peasants. The Black Five were the landowners, the rich, those deemed to have extreme right leanings, common criminals, and antirevolutionaries. Members of this group were frequently beaten and even executed. The Beijing Worker's Stadium was the scene of many public executions of suspected Black Five members.

Chinese families, and not just individuals, fit into this class system based on what was called the inheritance rule. It essentially stated, "The

As a member of the Black Five, I was considered to be the lowest form of human life, not worthy of living.

son is a hero if the father is a revolutionary. The son is a rotten egg if the father is an antirevolutionary." According to this rule, children were punished for the alleged sins of their parents.

I didn't have a chance. As a believer in Jesus Christ, I was automatically labeled as an antirevolutionary. As a member of the Black Five, I was considered to be the lowest form of human life, not worthy of living. The Black Five were considered to be the scum of the earth, and were denied all their rights in society. They were literally slaves for anyone who was a Communist Party member.

Since I had been a Party member myself, I was subjected to the most intense cruelty and was forced to work without pay. Whenever someone from the Communist Party told me to do something, I had to obey the order immediately and without question. If I disobeyed or delayed in carrying out the order in the precise manner the person preferred, I was publicly beaten and ridiculed. I felt like an animal. I felt like I was the scapegoat for everything that went wrong in China.

Obviously, the Black Five were not allowed to have a voice. We were forbidden to attend any meetings in which government policies were discussed or to have any influence on other members of our community. We were not even allowed to meet with each other in small private groups. We were considered to be the source of China's problems, and we all felt the burden of failure. Even after I was released from the labor camp, I was still marked as a member of the Black Five.

On the night I was released, I went straight to Brother Li's house. He was a very dear brother in the Lord, and I knew that he had been praying for me. I am convinced that the prayers of believers like Brother Li carried me through those hard times. Without the prayers of faithful brothers and sisters, I never would have survived. I dearly wanted to see Brother Li, so I traveled to Guaihe to meet with him.

During those days in China, no one had electricity, so people left their doors open at night to let in the cool air and starlight. I quietly slipped through the door and crept into the house, passing the family dog unnoticed. I could hear voices in the house praying. As I went into the room where everyone was praying, I paused to listen to their prayers.

They were all so caught up in the spirit of prayer that no one knew I was there. At that moment, they were praying for my release from the prison camp. I stood there and listened to their words of kindness, passion, and love for me. They had not forgotten me. They had not let me sit alone in prison but were with me in prayer.

As I listened, I could not help but start sobbing. Suddenly, everyone heard me crying, opened their eyes, and jumped up to embrace me. To be united with my brothers and sisters again was a dream come true.

It is not easy to explain to those who have never been in prison how I felt at that moment. I had spent so many nights praying for that event, night after night lying in bed wishing I could leave the horrors of the prison camp and wake up in the home of my family and friends. I had prayed that they would not forget me and that God would not forget them.

Above all, I had prayed that they would not forget their first love, Jesus Christ. Life could be unbearable for a member of the Black Five. At times, hope seemed out of reach, but I knew that His love would be faithful to the end.

After spending a little time with Brother Li and his fellowship, I left for another village about four miles away. Entering the village, I went to the home of another believer named Yaojie and her mother. When I walked around to the back of their house, I looked through the window and saw them praying. I tried to listen quietly to what they were praying before interrupting them.

I could hear them saying my name; they, too, were praying for my safety! I couldn't believe it. I tapped on the window, and they looked out at me, wondering who it might be. What a shock it must have been for them to see me peering through the window just as they were praying for me!

"It's me—Zhang!" I said as they opened the door, but they just stood there in astonishment. They could not believe that I was actually standing in front of them.

"It can't be you, can it? No. Brother Zhang?"

"Yes, it's me. Thank you for praying for me."

Those moments were so priceless. Again, it was truly a dream come true, as well as a very emotional scene.

I was full of energy after leaving Yaojie's house and could not stop thinking about going around and seeing all of my dear brothers and sisters. I ran to the next house, and then the next, to see everyone I had been thinking about during the entire time I was behind bars. I can remember being in the labor camp and looking up at the sky thinking about my brothers and sisters being in prayer meetings. I would also gaze at the sky and think about what it might be like for the Lord to return.

"Please come, Lord," I would pray. "Please come early. I need You. How I long for You to return this very moment. Please come this very moment and take me to be with You in the air, far from this earth."

During work hours, I had often written poems about gazing at the clouds. I had thought, *If only I could see Him come from heaven and rescue me from my enslavement!* Sometimes, the guards had caught me daydreaming and threatened to beat me if I didn't get back to work.

Even after I was released, I had to work for free. I had been labeled a member of the Black Five, and there was no way that I could shake that designation. I was forced to work on farms as a slave without pay. During those days, I had to work every day for as long as daylight lasted. There was no time for ministry. With my meager diet and the many hours I had to work out in the hot sun, I was always exhausted.

I was like a sheep working among a pack of wolves. They made everything difficult just to punish me even more for my belief in Jesus Christ. One day, when I was in the field, I was feeling very tired, and I yawned. I had no idea what kind of reaction my yawn would bring.

Everyone working around me immediately encircled me.

"This guy must be praying at night," someone yelled.

Over one hundred people swiftly ran over to where I was standing. Many of my coworkers and farm managers saw me as an enemy and wanted to see me suffer.

"He must be preaching to others when he is supposed to be resting! That is why he is tired!"

The rhetoric escalated in a matter of seconds, and then someone struck me. After the first blow, people started falling on me like an avalanche. Everyone was squeezing in to punch and kick me. I fell to the ground as they continued to beat me from head to toe. This went on until they wore themselves out and became bored of it.

They left me in immense pain. I burst into tears and was consumed with grief, wondering what made me so evil that others desired to make me suffer. Why was I so unlikable that others took glee in causing me pain? All I had done was yawn!

There was no rest from the persecution. On one occasion, during a rare break time in the field, a gang of thugs with no reverence for God asked me to join them. Their language was harsh and extremely offensive. I rejected their company because it would have required me to dwell on their words. They intentionally used provocative, disgusting language. They were the only people I'd met who could make an entire sentence out of profanity. Somehow, they managed to employ curse words as verbs, nouns, pronouns, adverbs—any part of speech.

When I refused to join them, they took it as a reason to be angry at me for not doing what they had ordered me to do. They became more and more aggressive, and I became quite angry and defended myself. "The words you speak dishonor yourself and women," I told them. "When you dishonor women, it is not just one woman but all women—including your mother. Your language dishonors your own mother who gave birth to you."

During the Cultural Revolution, there was no freedom of speech at all. There was not even the freedom to say biblical words like "hallelujah" out of habit. If other people heard you, you would be accused of attacking socialism. Just saying "hallelujah" could bring punishment and other consequences. I knew that there would be severe repercussions if I made any such outburst, but sometimes it was just a natural reaction.

One day, I wasn't thinking, and the word "hallelujah" slipped out of my mouth. It happened only once, and I thought there would be a bit of leeway. However, there were about thirty people standing around me at the time, and they immediately reacted by punching and kicking me to the ground.

One day, the word "hallelujah" slipped out of my mouth.

Thirty people standing around me immediately reacted by punching and kicking me to the ground.

In 1972, I got married. I'm really not sure how I was able to manage that under the circumstances. This event should have brought me a lot of happiness, but it didn't. I was sad and burdened, and it seemed to me that our wedding ceremony was covered in clouds. That year was not a good year for China. In fact, it had not been a great couple of decades for the struggling nation.

Unlike in the West, most Chinese do not choose whom they will marry. Most marriages are arranged either by families or—as is the case in underground house churches—by pastors. We also have matchmakers who help families find spouses for their young adults. We had a man in our village who was officially appointed to be the town matchmaker and who arranged local marriages. There was a lot of pressure on my wife and me to get married, and the matchmaker had made the arrangements when we were still very young.

At the time when our marriage was arranged, I lived at the top of the hill, and she lived at the bottom. She was not a Christian and had never even met one until she met me. She was part of a farming family, like I was, and it just made sense to the matchmaker that we should get married. We did not have a big Chinese wedding ceremony like many people have today. We were barely able to survive from day to day, so we did what other poor people did in those days—we simply went to the courthouse and filled out the paperwork. It was very uneventful.

I was given some time off to arrange the wedding, but the government was suspicious of my activities and sent agents to watch me and make sure that I didn't have a religious wedding ceremony. They also made sure that no Christian friends attended my wedding.

My wife is an amazing woman. When the matchmaker told her that he had arranged for her to marry me, the matter was settled in her mind. She committed herself to me from the beginning, knowing full well that she was marrying an antirevolutionary "enemy of the state." I brought a lot of burdens into the marriage because I was a Christian. For my part, I understood that I would suffer for my faith. Did not Christ Himself tell us to expect persecution? For my new wife, on the other hand, it was not as comprehensible because she was not even a Christian. But when she married me, she took on these additional burdens related to my faith in Jesus.

Our wedding took place in the midst of much suffering. Looking back, I truly wish we could have gotten married under better circumstances. To this day, I feel like that part of my life was stolen by the enemy.

8

Slaves of the Communist Party

After the wedding, I really wanted to settle down with my wife and live a normal life. I didn't want her to suffer because of me, but deep down inside, my soul was restless. The Lord had put a fire in my heart to preach the gospel, and that passion only increased the more I was persecuted.

The enemy of our souls had a burning passion, too; he longed to extinguish my life before God had a chance to use me. The first way he tried was through the local government officials in my hometown who wanted to destroy me. They felt that I had betrayed them, and they lashed out in hurt against me. They met together and devised a way to bring me to destruction.

The government officials in our county rounded up seventeen people who were labeled as Black Five members, myself included. We were considered to be the most offensive and disgusting antirevolutionaries in the nation. Again, the Black Five were the lowest of the low, and in the eyes of many people, we didn't deserve to live. Some Chinese found the Black Five so offensive that their existence alone was an affront to the revolution; they thought we should be executed on the spot. The passion of the students who were against the so-called antirevolutionaries ran high.

The police came to my village and arrested me in front of my home without offering any reason or giving any specific charges against me other than calling me an antirevolutionary. That was all that was needed. The accusation alone was conviction. The police took me to the center of town where I was lined up with the others and put on display. We were like trophies in the hands of the most zealous cadres. In their eyes, we were enemies of all that was good in society.

While we were made a public spectacle, it became clear that I was the youngest of the group. Most of the police officers were particularly displeased with me because I had not only betrayed the Communist Party but was young enough to know better. In their view, the older men were products of their own generation and needed only to be reeducated. Since I had been a Party member, I had no excuse for breaking the rules.

As I stood there, many different things went through my mind. I didn't know if we were just going to be marched through the street or publicly executed. Images of my grandfather being publicly flogged in a dunce cap came to mind.

One of the officers came out and announced our obligation. We were told to go up the mountain and dig a water reservoir by hand. We would not be paid because we were slaves of the Communist Party. It thus would not matter if we were injured in the process of building the reservoir. We were good for nothing other than free labor. If the government was able to use us for a good purpose prior to our starving to death or dying from injury, then it would be considered a good return on a minimal investment. At least society would have gotten every last drop of usefulness out of us.

It was not easy to get to the top of the mountain. We were force-marched by the local guard on duty. If we gave him any reason to kill us, he would do so without thinking twice, and no one would hold him responsible for our deaths. In fact, killing an antirevolutionary could even lead to a promotion.

Every day, we would make that climb, and I would always become incredibly parched halfway up the mountainside. We were given only the bare minimum of food and water necessary for survival. We didn't have enough water, so my body would cry out to me to stop. My tongue would swell from the effects of dehydration, and my lips would become dry and cracked. It would feel as if every part of me was desperately crying out for water. I would have done anything for a drink.

After the first day of labor on the mountain, my body ached from the laborious digging. The second time, going up the mountainside was twice as hard, but I knew that I didn't have a choice. My body went into survival mode, so I didn't feel much of anything other than the basic human instinct of self-preservation.

All seventeen of us worked together in a work gang. Our main job was to break up rocks, so our hands were ripped apart by the long hours of swinging sledge hammers and holding chisels. My bones were shaken to the point where every joint ached.

In those days, large bullhorns were placed in the centers of towns and cities throughout China so that important information could be announced to everyone at once. This was how it was announced to everyone in my township that the Black Five were at the top of the mountain building a new reservoir. We were a public spectacle, put on display for everyone to be reminded of what happens to those who don't march to the beat of the Party's drums.

People came to look at us as if we were zoo animals. They could not understand why someone so young would trade his life to follow superstition.

Word went around town that the Black Five were working on the mountainside. Most people were too poor to own radios in those days, and even those who did couldn't use them for entertainment purposes. Newspapers with the latest propaganda were an unnecessary expense, as well. (Sometimes, the daily newspaper was placed inside a glass case in the center of town or in the college areas so that it could be read for free by everyone.) Consequently, we members of the Black Five became the people's entertainment.

Groups of people would make a day of trekking up the mountain to see us. People came to look at us as if we were zoo animals. I remember them shaking their heads when they looked at me. They could not understand why someone so young would not join the revolution but would rather trade his life to follow superstition.

There wasn't any real reason for people to come up to the top of the mountain, but it became a popular destination for those who had idle time on their hands. Families and crowds of friends would stare at us for hours at a time. They would point at me and say to their children, "Look! There he is. There is the Jesus freak."

Sometimes, people would come by and shout things at me to see how I would respond. I felt like an animal in a cage who was being tortured by little children poking at it with sticks in order to get a reaction. The mocking went on hour after hour and day after day. I was not the only one being mocked and yelled at, but sometimes it certainly felt that way. I tried to stay strong and not let it get to me, but there were times when I was weak and felt like I had reached the end of my strength.

One day, one of the curious villagers who had trekked up the mountain to see me got close enough to ask me a question. He didn't know my name, but he didn't need to since I was just an object to most people, not a human being at all. He looked at me for a while until I noticed him standing there.

People usually talked about me with each other or just yelled at me, but almost no one actually engaged me.

"Hey," he said breaking the silence of his stare. "You used to be a Party member, didn't you?"

I nodded my head.

"Wow! Just look at you now. Do you ever regret your decision?"

I thought about the question and then responded, "I am here of my own choosing. No one forced me to take this path. It was my own feet that took me down this path, and this path will lead me to the cross of Jesus. It is not only my choice but my daily pursuit."

Immediately, I could tell that he was ready for my answer.

"But every day, people come to mock you and to see the shame that you have placed yourself in. How do you feel about that?"

I smiled at his question. I answered it not only for him but also for myself. "I feel that I am worth more today than ever before." It felt good to say that. I could tell that he was shocked by my statement.

"Before, people ignored me. They ignored the things that I said and the words that I spoke, but now people come from miles around to see me. They even make arrangements to take special trips to see me. Doesn't that alone prove that I am now more valuable than ever before?"

The man walked away dumbfounded.

In addition to the people from the village who come to gawk at me, my brothers and sisters in the Lord came to visit me. They would see the kind of torture I was going through, and they would weep for me. They were not allowed to speak to me, and I was not able to get a private moment with them so that we could share with each other. We were merely able to acknowledge one another through eye contact. That was not always easy, because sometimes they would be so hurt by what they saw that they were not able to stop crying long enough to look up and meet my gaze.

> Every true Christian in China was soon found out. The believers could not keep their light from shining in the darkness.

Many Christians during those days did not want their faith to be known because they did not want to endure what they saw me going through. The Party had struck fear into them. I knew of three Communist Party members who were secret Christians, just as I had been. They did everything they could to keep that fact quiet, but the truth eventually came out. Every true Christian in China was soon found out. The believers could not keep their light from shining in the darkness of China; it was like a beacon that could be seen from miles away. Those who were not truly passionate about their relationship with Jesus Christ had nothing to fear. They were not discovered by others because they did not really have anything to be discovered.

All seventeen of us Black Five members would work, eat, and sleep together as one group. Every night we would come down from the mountain. At first, we had enough energy to talk when no one was looking, and we made an effort to get to know one another; but after a short time, our energy was completely spent.

We were suffering from malnutrition and overexertion. It was the summer of 1973, and the sun shone down on us relentlessly every day. No one felt like moving more than was absolutely necessary. We would drop right to sleep as soon as we were able to. We had no energy left for late night conversation.

I remember lying on the ground at night before falling asleep. I waited for God to do a miracle. I waited for Him to rescue me out of the pits of hell. I clung to the stories of Daniel in the lion's den and Peter in prison with hope and anticipation that something miraculous would happen for me, as well. But after a while, I prayed only for Jesus' speedy return. I needed rest. I needed release. I needed Him.

The days were made even more unbearable for me by a man named Yifa Tian who was sent to our team as a monitor. Yifa had an unquenchable desire to see me suffer. I could feel the tension between us whenever he was around. I learned that his mother had been a Christian, but he rejected the faith wholeheartedly.

In 1969, his mother had borrowed a Bible from our church. Bibles were more precious than gold in those days. There were not many of them, and they could not be bought or reprinted anywhere. As more and more Bibles were confiscated and destroyed by the government, they became truly precious treasures.

When Yifa found out that his mother had borrowed a Bible, he took it and used it as toilet paper. He had a knack for being cruel to people that was evident in the way he dealt with me on a daily basis. Curses rolled off his lips every time he mentioned my name. All I could do was obey him and pray for him. I didn't hate him, but enduring his wickedness was a daily challenge.

Even one of the Black Five members named Brother Li mocked and cursed me until, one day, he felt an uncontrollable guilt come over him, and he came to me to apologize. Brother Li wept as he confessed all the ways in which he had mistreated me. Yifa noticed Brother Li crying and immediately demanded an explanation. There was nothing we could say to Yifa to help him understand what was happening in that moment.

"Are you, too, a Christian, Li?" Yifa demanded to know. Li didn't deny it but acknowledged by nodding his head.

"I can't believe it! Another one fooled into this garbage. What is it with you Christians? When will you ever learn?"

Yifa called over a group of men who were all too eager to cause us bodily harm. He demanded that Li be beaten and then taken to the local police station so that his crime could be recorded in the books.

Li's life was worth so little to Yifa. As I watched the cruel mob start to beat him, I couldn't help but want to save him. Watching the blood gush out of his body onto the ground was more than I could bear. In that moment, I had the unquenchable desire to kill everyone there who was hurting Li. I wanted to be like Moses when he saw an Egyptian beating an Israelite. I even began to imagine myself killing them and burying them in the sand, as Moses did with the Egyptian. (See Exodus 2:11–12.) In my moment of anger, I was able to maintain my sanity only by remembering the Lord's words that He alone is the righteous Judge. (See, for example, Romans 12:19.)

Even though I had thoughts of fighting back, I never actually did. It tormented me at times, but I always knew that the Lord would be my Protector. In that moment, it was Li who needed protection, but I knew that God would not forget him.

After a while, Yifa's time finally came. I had a dream one night in which a voice called out to me and said, "Today, the man who persecuted you will die." The dream was so vivid and clear. I woke up trembling and not really knowing what the dream meant. I have heard that most people dream every night, whether or not they remember their dreams, but this dream felt real and was still vivid in my mind after I awoke.

I went to breakfast that morning but was unable to stop thinking about my dream. With each bite, I just kept hearing the words, *Today, the man who persecuted you will die.* I pondered their meaning and tried to identify someone in particular who had persecuted me. The people who persecuted me were so numerous that it was truly not easy for me to single out one person.

Word was getting around that my God was alive and well and would protect me from my persecutors.

That day, I was told that I would be on a work detail that would cut out the side of the mountain with dynamite. We often worked with dynamite because of the level of danger involved. If one of the members of the Black Five work team were killed, it would not be much of a loss to the authorities.

I was told to report to the dynamite section of the work area after breakfast, but at the last minute, I received orders to report elsewhere. Yifa was sent to monitor the dynamite work detail, and he and the team went into the mountains without me. On one of the dynamite charges, a small stack and a large stack of explosives were put together. The large stack exploded, but no one noticed that the smaller stack had not. When Yifa moved in closer to inspect the explosion, the smaller stack suddenly exploded. Yifa's body was blown into pieces and strewn all over the area. Only about twenty kilograms (forty-four pounds) of his remains were recovered. Upon hearing the news, I was reminded of my dream the night before.

Because of China's tradition of superstitious beliefs, Chinese are naturally more superstitious than most. Immediately after Yifa's death, the others began to talk about the event. The more they discussed it, the more it became clear to them that this was Yifa's punishment for persecuting me. From that day onward, the team members were more careful about how they treated me.

Word was getting around that my God was alive and well and would protect me from my persecutors. People began saying, "Zhang believes in a true God. Jesus will protect Zhang from evil." Yifa's death had put a little fear of God in everyone.

The new leader of the Black Five team heard about the event and the rumors that were going around the camp. He, too, decided to treat me much better than I had been in the past. He even granted me permission to return home every weekend to spend time with my family—a rare privilege. I took advantage of the opportunity to go home every weekend and traveled around preaching at churches day and night.

It was such a wonderful experience to be back in the company of brothers and sisters in Christ. Wherever I went, people would welcome me with love and joy. It seemed that each church service was making a huge impact. Every meeting was filled with people coming to the Lord for salvation. Many would initially come to the meetings with critical attitudes, but the Word of the Lord would warm their hearts and overcome their cold spirits. Though times were not easy, God was blessing the preaching of His Word in a mighty way.

9

Li Tianen

During the time I worked in the Black Five labor gang, I really didn't know when the hell-on-earth would end. I didn't know if I would be there for another day, another month, or another year—or if I would be working on that mountain for the rest of my life.

I loved the time I spent with the church on the weekends, but in many ways it was additional work that drained all my energy before I returned to the backbreaking labor on the mountain. Spiritually, physically, and emotionally, I was utterly spent. I was physically tired and thirsty, but I also felt like I had not been spiritually fed for quite some time. I was at the end of my rope and running out of energy to feed others. I felt like the rich man in Jesus' parable who needed only a drop of water from Lazarus' finger in order to be quenched of thirst. (See Luke 16:19–31.) I was thirsty, and I cried out to God for spiritual water. I desperately needed rest and spiritual nourishment.

God answered my prayer. Brother Ma, a dear friend of mine who was a member of the Communist Party, shared my faith in Christ. He, too, had suffered much for the gospel. One night, Brother Ma slipped me a secret note. My heart jumped when I opened it.

The note said, "Midnight, come to Guipa Tao Village. A servant of God named Li Tianen is coming."

I immediately ate the note so that no one would catch me with it. As I stood there, my heart began to jump with joy. Teaching from Li Tianen was exactly what I needed.

Like me, Li Tianen was born in Fangcheng County, Henan Province, but he had spent most of his life in Shanghai. He belonged to the generation of Christians before me, having been born in 1928, and he came from a long lineage of faithful believers. His grandfather was converted by the missionary Hudson Taylor, the famed founder of the China Inland Mission.

Li had been brought up by his mother, who was a traveling evangelist, but she died shortly after the Japanese invaded China. Li was only nine years old at the time, and he was sent to live with his grandparents. Later, he attended the Baptist seminary in Kaifeng, Henan Province.

I was excited to sit under the teaching of Pastor Li. It was not common to have a formally trained pastor in the area, so it was a big deal whenever he came to Henan. Pastor Li had a church outside of Shanghai, and he was more Shanghainese than Henanese. The government had tried to force Li to renounce the name of Jesus Christ, but he had refused; consequently, he had been sent to prison in Anhui Province, where he had been tortured in the most inhumane manner. Upon his release, he had immediately traveled back to Henan Province to plant churches and to evangelize the area of Fangcheng in response to a letter from believers in Henan asking him to come preach.

As I prepared to sneak out of the camp to hear Pastor Li speak, I remembered to put some bread in my pocket. The bread was not for me to eat. I kept it so that I could give it to the dogs if they came out after me. It would give them something to do with their mouths so they would not bark at me and alert the villagers that someone was secretly passing down their road. Due to my extreme hunger, it was tremendously difficult for me not to eat the bread, but my spiritual hunger was much greater.

The night I went to hear him speak was truly one of the best evenings of my life. As I'd thought, Pastor Li's teachings were exactly what I needed. They fed my hungry soul. I hung on every word and tried to take mental notes of every gospel example on which he elaborated.

Pastor Li was a very gentle man, but he preached with deep passion. It was clear that the Lord had anointed him. Everyone who heard him speak felt that his message was coming from God. I could feel myself getting stronger and stronger just listening to Pastor Li preach.

I even recall the message he shared that night. It was about Mary using her precious perfume for Jesus. He told how Mary broke the jar of expensive perfume in hopes that it would please her Lord. (See, for example, John 12:3–8.) "Too many believers today have been given expensive jars of perfume, but they refuse to break them. They are hanging on to them, but they don't know for what reason. Love for Jesus requires complete surrender. Hold nothing back. Nothing is more precious, nothing is more valuable, than the Savior being with us. We are to hold nothing back."

> "Love for Jesus requires complete surrender. We are to hold nothing back."

As I sat there, I realized that I could not hold anything back. After hearing his words, I silently prayed, *Lord, my life is all I have to offer to You. It is not an expensive bottle of perfume, but I break it willingly before You. May the contents of this broken jar be an acceptable fragrance to You, O Lord.*

I did not know it then, but Pastor Li was going to be a major mentor in my life. We would also travel a lot together in the future.

That night, we were able to sit down and talk together. He shared with me about his time in the Anhui prison. He told me about the ways in which the Lord had kept him safe and had looked after him during his ten-year sentence. He also shared with me about miracles he had experienced under the direst conditions.

He recalled how he was once piling up stones in a quarry on the edge of a dangerous cliff. As he was moving rocks, he took a wrong step and fell more than thirty feet to the bottom of the cliff. All the other prisoners thought that he had died. He had an out-of-body experience in which he watched what was going on as his body was taken to the doctor. He had soared above his body like an eagle, but he knew that it wasn't his time to go. His body was not breathing and didn't show any signs of a pulse. The prisoners opened his eyes and could see that there was no life in him. The doctor then examined his body; after ninety minutes, he determined that Li was dead and ordered the other prisoners to prepare a grave.

Just then, Li opened his eyes and looked at the doctor. The doctor was completely amazed that he was looking into Li's eyes and asked him if he knew who he was. He responded that his name was Li Tianen, and he asked the doctor if he believed in God, to which the doctor replied, "I believe in God now."

As I sat there listening to all the hardships that Pastor Li was describing, I was able to identify with him. His stories and testimonies made my spirit leap with joy and strengthened me.

Pastor Li then told me of another time when the prison had assigned two prisoners to watch him and ensure that he didn't move his lips to pray. If they saw any signs that he was praying, they were ordered to torture him.

One of the men discovered the secret hiding place in Pastor Li's bedding where he hid his Bible. He immediately called out to the watch commander on duty. As the commander came to inspect Li's bed for his Bible, a call came through that needed his immediate attention. He went away, and Li's Bible was never found.

Pastor Li made spiritual deposits into my spirit that I would carry with me for many years. I didn't know it then, but every bit of encouragement would be necessary. The hardest trials were ahead of me, and I needed all the strength and inspiration I could get.

10

"Satan's Camp": The Mouth of the Dragon

As Chinese New Year 1974 came to an end, the government's focus on my outreach activities had reached a flat point, and I was given some breathing room. Additionally, after my time with Pastor Li, I really felt encouraged and strengthened to face the coming challenges with joy. If my Lord found me worthy enough to trumpet His name in the most horrendous situations, then I felt that it would be an honor to do so. Although I had felt my strength fleeing from my body during the early days of hard labor, my energy was back now. I felt like I had just received my second wind.

In March 1974, every household in Fangcheng County that was accused of being Christian was put on a list. This list was compiled from prior arrests and then handed to the government officials in charge of putting together work parties. Mao Zedong had a vision to build roads that stretched across all of China, connecting places that had never before been connected to the rest of the country. Henan was commissioned to build more roads in order to increase national commerce by speeding up the process of shipping goods for both business concerns and military efforts.

Everyone on the list in Fangcheng County was called up to begin working on road construction, providing free labor for the government. Even my sixty-year-old grandmother was forced to go out and build roads. I found out that I was not on that list and thus was not among those forced to build roads for the government.

I was actually hurt that my name was not on the list. I know this might sound strange to a Westerner, but it felt like I had been cheated when I learned that I was not considered worthy enough to be on the Fangcheng list of Christians forced to be slave labor.

I cried out to the Lord, "God, what have I done to not be on that list? I have faithfully followed You and proclaimed Your name. Please don't allow this persecution to pass me by. Don't allow someone else to suffer in my place. I will gladly show the world that I am committed to You."

In that moment, the Lord comforted me. I was instantly taken away in the Spirit by His supernatural grace, and I heard Him say to me, "My child, be patient. Something else will be coming your way. You have been measured, and your cross has been prepared."

I was confused, but the word of the Lord provided me with comfort. I did not need to be comforted for very long, because I received a letter from the local government on May 3, 1974. It reprimanded me, informing me that I was a counterrevolutionary and would be required to attend reeducation classes specifically set up for religious people. Chairman Mao's wife, Qing Jiang, was determined to eradicate Christianity from China forever and was the main force behind the institution of these classes.

My heart jumped for joy. Before I had even reached the end of the letter, I ran home as fast as I could. I went running into my mother's house with the letter held high in my hand, shouting, "Mother! Mother! You need to see this letter. God heard my prayer! God heard my prayer!"

Those who follow the Lord must be a bit insane by the world's standards. No one could note the humble way in which Jesus came into the world and think that this was the manner by which God would bring His kingdom to earth. How could the King of the universe be born in a barn? How could the Creator of all living things be raised in the home of a common carpenter with no formal religious education? No one could think about the torture of Christ, including the crown of thorns that was placed on His head, and truly believe that this was part of God's original plan for the salvation of humanity since before the fall of man. No one could look at Jesus' death on the cross and understand with worldly reasoning how that was a victory.

Similarly, it would be impossible for me to explain to an unbeliever the pain of being excluded from punishment when other believers were enduring hardship in my place. It might not even be possible to explain it to the comfort-seekers found in many churches today! I was excited because I had been chosen as one worthy enough to identify with my Savior in suffering. That meant that I would also be identified with Him one day in glory! (See, for example, Hebrews 2:9–10.)

I'm glad I didn't know then what I would soon come to learn. The classes that I was told to attend were not academic courses with lectures and a test at the end of the semester. I was heading into the mouth of the dragon. I was walking into the darkest dungeon that I had ever experienced in all my life.

> **We were at the point of no return. Everyone around us had been trained to brainwash us.**

The classes soon became known among the Christians as "Satan's Camp." I would be repressed, starved, and tortured; I would suffer from diseases that I had never even heard of. The "classes" were meant to either change me or kill me, and the atmosphere was little better than that of a Holocaust-era concentration camp. The shadow of death lingered over us like a vulture, and we were intimidated by the ever-present reality that our lives held little value in the government's eyes.

Four of us from the local area—Huifang's mother; Guizhen Jia, one of my spiritual mothers; Jibin Lou; and myself—were told to report to the classes. We met together beforehand and prayed for one another. We encouraged each other to stay strong and never to deny the name of Jesus. "In all things, we must stand strong. In all things, let us glorify the name of Jesus," I said.

As we walked together through the camp's entrance, I felt a strong presence of despair in the air. The guards who had heard about me shook their heads. They were completely disgusted at the sight of me because they knew that I used to be a leader in the Communist Party.

We were at the point of no return. Everyone around us had been trained to brainwash us. The guards circled us like lions around their prey. Things began to happen fast. I was quickly tied up, and then kicks and punches came from every direction. In the heat of the moment, I tried to bring my knees up to guard my midsection. I closed my eyes tighter with each blow. Suddenly, I could taste warm blood in my mouth. The guards were wildly swinging their fists and yelling, and I could hear the other prisoners screaming while absorbing the blows. It was a barrage of violent rage.

In all, thirty of us were tortured in this way. It was hard to know what everyone else was going through because of the cacophony of blows and screams.

"Where is your Bible, Christian?" the guard asked me.

I didn't respond.

"Where is your Bible, Christian?" As I closed my eyes from the pain, I heard others screaming.

"Oh, you will talk. You will talk!"

Above all the yelling and screaming, I could hear the crack of a whip. The sharp sound cut through the air. The next swing ripped into my flesh.

"Where is your Bible? Where do you Christians meet? What songs do you sing? Where are your leaders?"

The questions were rapidly fired at me between each lash of the whip. It was not long before I began to hear other prisoners break. No one had passed out, and the only thing they could do to stop the pain was to deny the name of Jesus, and so they did. Those in the camp who denied Jesus had to prove it to the authorities by identifying other believers. They were immediately forced to write down the names of those whom they knew to be practicing Christians.

The guards wanted me to deny Jesus, too, but that was never an option. Although I wanted to die, the torture was only beginning. I wanted the beatings to stop, but nothing in my power could make that happen.

Needless to say, after the beatings finally stopped, I was in excruciating pain. That night, I tried to feel for broken bones, but it was hard to tell what might be broken. Even the slightest attempt to move shocked my system with pain. I just wanted to lie still. I prayed to the Lord to take the pain away. At first, I had been concerned about the dirt from the ground getting into the open wounds on my body, but now I didn't care. I didn't have the energy to do anything about it.

On May 5, we were brought out to the prison yard. A special sign was made and placed around my neck. It said, "Beat Zhang Rongliang, who opposes the revolution." The sign hanging from my neck was an order directly from the leaders to the prisoners to beat me. Anyone who killed me would be let out of prison. No one would get in trouble for taking my life. In fact, it would be a dishonorable thing if I passed by and someone showed compassion for me.

I begged the Lord to take my life. I never knew how much pain I was capable of feeling.

I dragged myself through the streets inside the camp as people yelled at me, spit on me, kicked me, and threw things at me. I couldn't stop because that would have meant certain death. The only way I could survive was to keep on moving through the mob, no matter how much it hurt. My hands were black from the dirt and mud, and my face was red with blood. The pain was indescribable.

That night, I no longer wanted to live. I begged the Lord to take my life. I never knew how much pain I was capable of feeling. Initially, I had arrogantly thought that I was tough and would be able to handle it, but I couldn't. We were beaten at least three times every day, and every room was filled with terror.

I could hear the cries of people calling out for their parents. I could hear men screaming for their mothers. People yelled, "Stop" and "Help" over and over. But no one came to help, and the guards certainly didn't stop until they felt like it. More than anything else, I heard people crying out to God.

Formerly, my greatest prayer had been that God would use me in any way He wanted to. Now my greatest prayer was simply to die.

Out of the thirty of us who were sent to be reeducated, only four survived without denying the name of Jesus. We continued to encourage each other whenever we were able to, and we always exalted the name of Christ.

The four of us were classified as rebellious and referred to in the camp as stubborn rebels. Even though the pain was intense, over time, we felt stronger than the guards who were beating us. We would say something like this to them: "Maybe you can get others to deny Jesus, but I will not deny Him. How can I? He is all that I have. You have taken away everything else, so I have nothing left. I have no one else but Jesus. He will not deny me, and I cannot deny Him. Even though the entire town denies Him, I will not."

The guards shook their heads. They felt that we were just too rebellious.

By May 11, I was still in shock. Everything in me screamed with pain. I had never known such depths of human evil. I had previously been so ignorant of the breadth of human anger.

That morning, while moving from the place where they fed us, I saw a human figure lying on the side of the road outside our building. When I got closer, I saw that it was my spiritual mother, Guizhen Jia. She was a meek and loving woman who was always praying for others. Whenever I was tired, weak, or confused, she would encourage me and pray for me. And she had been like a mother to our church, as well.

Now, she was only a shell of who she used to be. Her hair was wildly matted to her head, where there were patches of bald spots. Her shirt, which clearly used to be white, was covered in dried blood. Her face had been disfigured by massive bruising, and blackened by coal and dirt. She looked like she had been dragged down the road.

Guizhen Jia was not able to stand. She had been thrown into a crowd that had beaten her over and over again. They had ripped off her shoes and stomped on her feet until some of her toes came off.

My mouth was so swollen that it wasn't possible for me to speak to her. I didn't know how to comfort her. I felt inadequate to protect this wonderful woman who was a mother of two and had recently become a grandmother. I ran to her and tried to embrace her. There were no words. I held her in my arms and wept bitterly.

Finally, I said, "Let us die together. Let us be buried together."

One of the guards heard me say this and ran over and kicked me under the chin. The swift kick lifted me up and onto my back. Several others ran to assist the guard. They dragged my body over to a tree. My legs were too weak to stand, so they used a rope to tie me to its trunk.

"How dare you openly defy us in broad daylight? Do you know where you are right now? Your God is not here, but we are. We are the gods of this town."

Take me away, dear Lord, I prayed silently to myself. I kept looking up to the sky, waiting for the Lord to come and take me. I could feel that I was losing consciousness, but it wasn't happening fast enough. My spiritual strength was decaying more and more every day. I had no more strength left and just wanted the Lord to come back and take me home.

That night, after I was dragged back to the room where we all slept, I was tossed onto the dirt floor and left for dead. I had been beaten and was barely alive, but I was still breathing. The May heat made our room like a furnace at night because there was no way for the cool air of the evening to flow into our cell.

No one in the room had been allowed to bathe or wash at all. Lying there in the night, I could hear the groaning and crying. I was not alone. Everyone was suffering. In many ways, I had it easy. I had not lost any limbs, nor had I suffered a bad concussion like many of the others had.

In the dark of night, I could hear the voice of one of the men in the room. His name was Lanju Gao. He was a Muslim and the most educated person in the room. He had graduated from high school.

"Zhang? Can you hear me?" Lanju whispered.

I waited a moment. I had to breathe so that I could answer him without pain. "Yeah," I replied. I didn't know if he heard me or not. If the guards heard us talking, they would certainly come storming back in.

"I saw what they did to you today." I could hear the pain in his voice. "I saw them tie you up to the tree, and…I saw everything. Zhang? Do you think I can believe in your God?"

"Zhang? Do you think I can believe in your God?"

I was dumbfounded. I was not only weak but at a loss for words. I had been so consumed with my own pain and my own situation that I had never thought it would be possible to share Christ with someone. I felt inadequate. I wanted to give up, even to die. How could God possibly use me to share His life and truth when all I wanted was death and escape?

"I saw you today, Zhang, and I believe that you serve the one true God."

"All you have to do is believe in Jesus. Call upon Him, and you will be saved."

In the darkness of that furnace-like room, I heard him cry out to Jesus that night. My strength was renewed.

11

Religious Criminal

Not long after Lanju became a Christian, the guards caught him praying. Lanju was already in trouble and didn't need anything more against him. He bravely told them that he had become a Christian.

The guards didn't know what to do. Their goal was to turn Lanju into an atheist and make him deny his faith. It was completely unfathomable to them that he had actually become a Christian in their camp. They were not only angry but also afraid. If word got out that people were coming to their atheist indoctrination camp and finding Jesus, they might lose their jobs or even their lives.

The guards scrambled to rectify the situation as quickly as possible. They tied Lanju up, beat him, and barraged him with questions. All they could get out of him was, "Jesus is the real God! Jesus is the real God!" There was nothing they could do to make him stop saying that.

"What makes you so certain that Jesus is God?" they asked.

They had to wait for Lanju to catch his breath before he had the strength to answer. "Because," he said with great pain, "because I watched how you beat Zhang Rongliang. I watched him get beaten even though he was innocent of any crime. You beat him, and he took it all. He took everything that you had to dish out and never complained. When I watched him, there was a peace and strength in him that convinced me that he serves the one and true God. I have turned from the darkness, and now I walk in the light."

He paused for a moment, and then he lifted up his head and said, "Now I serve the one and true God, too."

The guards released him, but they didn't untie his hands. They left them tied up behind his back so tightly that it was cutting off his circulation. I was unable to untie his hands, but I fed him the first chance I got. I could see that he had truly changed; he was no longer the same person. The beatings had not gotten him down but had rather convinced him even more that God was alive and would protect him.

He looked up at me and said, "It is sad that I am the only one here speaking with you right now, Zhang. I know that if there were one hundred people in this room right now, there would be no way for them not to do what I have done. I know they would all give their lives to Christ. They would all repent, because the love of Christ is so strong right now that no one could resist it." This is what the apostle Paul meant when he said that our gospel witness is *"to one a fragrance from death to death, to the other a fragrance from life to life"* (2 Corinthians 2:16).

He shook his head as he struggled to swallow the food. "I know that the love of Christ will one day win over the hearts of the Chinese people. Our county will one day come to know the love of Jesus and will be set free from this evil darkness."

It was amazing, but in that moment, during his darkest hour, Lanju was prophesying over China. He did not know that one day China would have the world's largest revival. Lanju later became a great evangelist and turned many people away from the false religion of Islam to Christ.

What we had called "Satan's Camp" lasted for only twenty days, but it felt like years. The brainwashing classes came to an end, and many people were sent home. I was not one of them. On June 10, a police officer came to me with one last plea. I could tell that the guards were getting exhausted and had run out of ideas. I had made their life difficult. They could have moved on, been promoted, and started working on several other things instead of spending all their energy on converting me. I felt sorry for them. They could have saved themselves so much time if they had believed me when I told them in the beginning that I would not deny Christ. Instead of spending so many nights with me, they could have spent that time with their families.

"Rongliang," the officer said to me as he came into the room, "you are still so young. You still have your entire life ahead of you. Why would you risk it all and throw it away by opposing the government? You have a nice home in the quiet mountainside and aging family members who need your care. You cannot care for them from the inside of a jail cell."

There was a moment of sincerity in his voice as he reflected on my choices, but then he straightened up, looked at me, and earnestly made his one final plea. "This is your last chance. All you have to say is 'I no longer believe,' and I will let you go home tomorrow." Then his expression changed as he continued, "But Zhang, if you refuse, I will have no choice but to send you off to prison."

I had been threatened so many times that I was used to it by that point. No one had lied to me. Everyone who had threatened me had told me the truth. They had said that each stage would be harder, and they had told me that each imprisonment would be avoidable. But what they had failed to understand was that giving in and denying the name of Jesus would have been worse than any earthly prison or pain I could imagine. What they did not know is that my pain was finite but the glory of being with my Savior would be forever.

> "This is your last chance. All you have to say is 'I no longer believe,' and I will let you go home tomorrow."

"You could ask me a thousand times, but my answer will always be the same. I will never deny the name of Jesus," I said. With that, the officer left in a rage.

Three days later, on June 13, 1974, Wentian Guo came to me at nine in the morning and told me that it was time to go. "Congratulations," he said mockingly. "You have graduated. You have completed Satan's Camp, and now you will be taken to prison."

I was too tired and in too much pain to respond.

I had to walk from the camp to the local prison. Before I was ushered out, I stopped and looked around. It was not easy to go. I was leaving behind so many close friends. The people at Satan's Camp were more than just acquaintances I had made during incarceration. They were my family; we were like brothers and sisters.

As I walked out, I started to cry. I knew that I might never again see some of the brothers and sisters who had stood beside me during those dark days of "reeducation classes." Something inside of me broke at the thought of never embracing them again on this side of eternity. During the hardest beatings and the darkest hours of my life, I didn't shed a single tear. But as I was walking away from my friends, I found myself weeping uncontrollably.

The walk from the camp to the prison took about twenty minutes. When I arrived, I was taken into custody, and a certificate of confession was put in front of me.

"Read this and sign it," ordered the officer.

I looked at the paper and read, "Zhang Rongliang, a religious criminal, has committed the crime of an antirevolutionary."

I signed my name, admitting to the crime, and walked into the prison.

Dear Lord, I prayed, *I really need relief. If possible, please let me find Brother Chen.* I had heard that a brother named Chen Hai Lu, who was well-known for preaching the Word of God, had been arrested and had been put in the same prison I was in. There was a rumor that he had arrived nine days earlier. I had no way to confirm the rumor, but I prayed that somehow God would put us together. I was spiritually weak and needed his fellowship. I knew that life would be easier to bear if I could only spend some time with Brother Chen.

The prison guard led me down the corridor and stopped in front of the compartment that would become my new home: Cell #10. And there in front of me was the cheerful face of Chen Hai Lu! He had been assigned to help me with my belongings. My heart leaped. I could not let on how happy I was to see Brother Chen because the guards would immediately have been furious. I did all I could to contain myself.

Once we were alone together, we were able to pray for each other and encourage one another. It was exactly what I needed. For me, that prison cell was like paradise. I never could have imagined that things would work out so well for me as to be assigned Brother Chen as a cellmate. For a brief moment, it was as if I was not even in prison anymore.

12

Winter Sweet

Like everywhere else in China during 1974, food was scarce in Henan Province. It was even harder to obtain when you were behind bars. Most of the inmates were wasting away from starvation, and Brother Chen was no exception. It could not have been easy for the prison to find food for the prisoners in those days because it is never easy to justify feeding lawbreakers when so many law-abiding citizens are dying of starvation.

We ate noodles every day, which, as I mentioned previously, are the most common staple in Henan. We often say that noodles are the Henan people's rice. Our food was rationed out, and we were supposed to receive a specific amount per person according to prison rules, but the guards often stole from our rations so that we received only a portion of the allotted amount. The noodles they fed us every day were black and tasteless, not to mention void of any nutrition. Everyone was malnourished, and Brother Chen's health was deteriorating day by day.

I spent time praying with him and shared my food with him, but I could see that he was getting weaker. As I prayed with him and tried to encourage him, I could feel my own body weakening. I started to have problems with my lungs, as well.

I often sang songs to ease the pain. I would sing loudly enough for Chen to hear, but softly enough to avoid the guard's notice. I remember looking out the window of the prison cell, wondering if I would survive. There were times when my faith was strong and I could feel the sweet presence of the

Lord, but there were other times when I would contemplate where I would be buried. I would look out onto the graveyard close to the prison and wonder if that was where I would end up.

Historically, Chinese culture has been based on loyalty, honor, and commitment, but somehow our culture had deteriorated to the point that self-interest and self-preservation were more important.

As the days went by, food rations got even tighter. When food became scarcer, fights among the prisoners over food became more frequent. Many of the prisoners began acting like rabid dogs. If they didn't receive enough food, they would snarl at the server. If someone reached into someone else's bowl or took another person's share of food, he would be mercilessly assaulted. Some prisoners would eat their food as fast as they could and then viciously try to steal from others.

The entire Chinese population seemed to be turning into animals. Human life had no value, and men and women were giving in to their base instincts to kill or be killed, eat or be eaten. The fact that Chen and I shared our food willingly with one another shocked everyone. No one understood it. As they were ripping through each other like sharks in a feeding frenzy, Chen and I were praying over our food, breaking bread together, and sharing with each other.

After witnessing our love for one another, some of the prisoners came to the Lord. Among those who gave their lives to Christ in prison after observing Chen and me were Jinxin Liu and Zhaolai Wang. Liu and Wang became dear brothers, and we were all able to avoid the dishonest system of the prison and rely on one another. We had our own subculture of love and loyalty that superseded our own interests and overpowered our own instincts for self-preservation.

Historically, Chinese culture has been based on loyalty, honor, and commitment. Children and the elderly alike were prized and cherished from generation to generation in old China, but somehow—almost overnight—our culture had deteriorated to the point that self-interest and self-preservation were more important than the lives of even our own parents or children.

Despite the collapse of society all around us, Chen and I remained loyal to one another. We did not betray each another, and we always placed our own self-interest secondary to the interests of the other. The hardships of that prison brought Chen and I closer together. We suffered together and watched out for one another, and we developed a strong bond like that of David and Jonathan. (See 1 Samuel 17:55–18:4.)

As 1974 skulked along, the darkness became thicker. The crackdown on Christians in China became more focused as officials were rewarded whenever they captured Christians. One of the more well-known preachers in Tanghe County was eighty-one-year-old Huaru Wang. He was a faithful servant of God who had given his entire life to share the gospel of Jesus. The police arrested him and brought him to our prison; they knew that he was elderly and weaker than the rest of us, but they still treated him mercilessly.

A few months later, other Fangcheng County church leaders were arrested, as well. Yunjiu Gao had been arrested four times before, and he was a bit of a mystery to most people. He was one of the few people who seemed actually to be energized by his arrests. It was almost as if his spirit fed off imprisonment. It was truly an odd thing.

In October, Guizhen Jia, my spiritual mother, was also arrested and brought to the same prison where I had been placed. Remarkably, she had survived "Satan's Camp" after having been practically beaten to death. It was selfish of me to enjoy her presence, but I did. I loved the stories she told and the encouragement she gave to us all. Before the end of 1974, a large raid brought approximately eighteen preachers into the prison from the churches in Fangcheng County. Among them were well-known men like Yudong Chen, Qingshan Lu, Genfa Zhao, Fengchen Li, Fuzhang Qiao, and David Zhou.

As the number of Christians in the prison grew, our expectations for the miraculous also increased. We rejoiced with each new brother or sister brought into the prison because it meant greater fellowship. To the guards, we must have seemed like fools with bleak futures, but we knew that we were children of the King of Kings. Little did they know that we considered it an honor to suffer for Christ. Many could not understand this until the day that they, too, received Christ as their Lord and Savior.

Even though the guards set the rules at the prison, they could not keep the hearts of the believers imprisoned.

The prison guards allowed us to walk outside for a few minutes every day to get some sun and fresh air, but speaking with other inmates was strictly forbidden. None of us was allowed to communicate openly, so we came up with signals in order to share with one another. We would also write Scripture passages under our sleeves and then reveal them when we passed one another so that we could encourage each other with the Word of God.

One day, I made the mistake of speaking out loud to Brother Gao when I saw him pass by. Almost immediately, a guard nearby drew his knife and came at me. I turned away from him to shield my face, and he slashed the back of my head with the blunt side of the blade. Another day, Huaru Wang shared about Jesus with another inmate out loud and was beaten for half a day to the point that I thought he was going to die.

The guards were also going through a lot of difficulties, and they tortured us as a means of working out their frustrations. Almost every day, the guards would pull me from my cell and put my head and arms into a freestanding wall that was designed to hold prisoners in place, similar to stocks. My wrists would be inserted through holes in the wall, along with my head, and then the top would be closed upon them, separating my head and hands from the rest of my body. After I was secured into the wall, the guards would poke me in the face over and over again with bayonets.

Even though the guards set the rules at the prison, they could not keep the hearts of the believers imprisoned. We found ways to find fellowship with one another and were thus able to rise above all our problems. There was nothing that could hold us back from our freedom in the Lord.

We were not allowed to have visitors or see our families, but we never lost hope. We knew that God would not ignore our cries forever, nor would He allow us to suffer beyond our limits. When one of us felt like giving up, the rest of us would rally together to lift up that person before the Lord. There was no judging or strife among us. We all had our strong points and our weak points, but this was no time for quarrels.

Our biggest problem was finding a satisfactory way to communicate. One day, Yanjiu Gao came up with a plan that would help to keep us all connected and inspired. "Zhang," Yanjiu whispered, "I have an idea. How about digging a secret tunnel to share messages between us throughout the week?"

"What?" I asked. It didn't make sense. How could we dig tunnels in the prison when we were being monitored all day, every day?

He crouched down a little lower and whispered, "You know how we take our sheets out to wash them and dry them every Saturday?"

"Yes, and...?" I didn't know what that had to do with anything.

"You know what my sheets look like, and I know what yours look like," he continued. "You can write a note and insert it into your own sheet sleeve. I can do the same, and when we come out to get our sheets, we can just take each other's."

I understood then that he wasn't talking about digging anything but about a way to pass information between us. The very first time we did this, it felt invigorating. I would read the brief letters from Yanjiu whenever no one else was around and I was able to find time. As we got better at it, we began to write mini-journals describing things that had happened during the week and some of the thoughts and challenges we were going through. This allowed us to better understand each other and pray for one another, and it gave us an outlet to share our thoughts and frustrations with another human being.

Before long, other believers were joining us by sending notes to each other using their sheets. We were completely surrounded by our enemies, but these notes were our lifeline. They allowed us to write the things that we had been thinking but had been unable to communicate. Through these sheet notes, we were able to have fellowship. We rejoiced when we read about a victory of one of our brothers, and we were inspired when a brother shared what the Lord had been sharing with him.

These notes also changed the way we looked at each other when we met in passing. Our earlier attempts to communicate ideas, encouragement, and support through gestures, half-whispers, and eye movements were not nearly as fruitful as this "tunnel." Now we could just look at someone and almost tell what he was thinking because of the things he had written to us. It was as if you knew something about each person's heart. In some ways, it was even more intimate than words, because some of us would write things on paper that we might never express verbally in front of others. Writing also allowed us time to reflect on our own circumstances. While it is easy to get sidetracked and ramble on during a conversation, putting things down on paper helped us to focus on our thoughts and reflections.

Like everything else in prison, this newfound freedom of expression came with a price. One day, a prison guard caught Brother Huaru reading his note from the sheets. The officer demanded that he hand it over, but instead of doing so, Huaru quickly ate the note. Huaru's deliberate disobedience of prison authority enraged the other officers, and they announced that he would be beaten for his act of insubordination. I heard that he was going to be beaten until he was "half-dead."

As concerned as I was for Huaru, something about that phrase "half-dead" made me think. In the past, every time the guards wanted to beat a prisoner, they would promise to beat him *to death*. And whenever the prisoners commented on the beating of another prisoner, they would say that the officers beat him *to the point of death*. The way that Huaru's beating was described struck a note in me, telling me that things were about to change for the better.

I was filled with hope and sent a letter to Gao, saying, "There is hope. I believe our church is about to experience a revival. I heard today that

Huaru would be beaten 'half to death,' which tells me that a change is coming."

Gao wrote back, "It was such a comfort to receive your letter today. I believe you are right. Being 'half-beaten' is like getting a fresh olive leaf from the mouth of a dove after being aboard the ark with Noah. It predicts that the disaster is about to pass and the land will turn green again!"

I read Gao's note over and over and held it close to my chest each time I finished reading it. I didn't have many things of my own in prison, but I had hope. During those long days, by means of the "secret tunnel," we communed, inspired each other, rejoiced, and kept growing in the Lord. Just as Paul wrote about his experiences, *"we [were] afflicted in every way, but not crushed; perplexed, but not driven to despair; persecuted, but not forsaken; struck down, but not destroyed"* (2 Corinthians 4:8–9).

I didn't have many things of my own in prison, but I had hope.

I lay down in my prison cell and stared at the cracks in the dusty concrete ceiling above. No one could have known the level of excitement that was shooting through my body at that time. Usually, flowers bloom in the spring, so everyone watches for springtime to see them. But there is one flower in China that blooms during the darkest portion of the winter. A direct translation of the Chinese name for this flower is "winter sweet." It is a special blossom because when all the northern regions of China are covered in snow and enduring the longest nights and the harshest weather, this one flower has the audacity to brave the storms and grow. The perseverance of this stubborn flower brings beauty in the darkest hour. Likewise, only the children of God can bring beauty during the most difficult hours of human history. Only the church can bring light to a world that is dark and dying.

I shared a cell with fellow prisoners Jinxing Liu, Guoqing Li, and Zhaolai Wang. They all had become believers while in prison. I asked them why they had chosen the darkest hour for Christians in China to place their faith in Christ. This was their reply: "During this whole year, we saw Jesus through your life, love, and action. You didn't preach with words but with actions. When we saw the way you behaved, we felt a power that we could describe only as love. Your faithfulness to your Lord is beyond death. None of us wanted to be here in prison, but thanks to this horrible situation, we were given a chance to see and to feel the Lord's greatness and abounding love."

I was in my early twenties at this time and did not think I would live much longer, but I knew that there might be a chance for me to make a difference in this world. My first son was born in 1975, while I was in prison. He was being raised by my wife, who was not yet a Christian. However, I didn't worry. Somehow, I knew that my son would one day grow up to be used by God.

Unfortunately, my wife did not have an opportunity to know what it was like to have a husband at home. She didn't share my faith in Jesus Christ, and I could not blame her for being angry at me for not being home or providing for our family. It was hard to see so many people in prison come to Christ while she remained unrepentant, but I had no other choice than to believe that one day she, too, would be saved.

13

On the Verge of Death

The years 1974–1976 were the peak of the Cultural Revolution, and these three years were an extremely tough period in China. People were dying every day from starvation, exposure, or government persecution. Although many authors around the world have written books with firsthand testimonies of that time in an attempt to capture its pain and turmoil, the magnitude of the nationwide pain and tragedy can never really be known. In those days, it felt like we were living on the verge of death every day, like a lamb being led to slaughter. Purely by the grace of God, I survived that time and lived to tell about it.

In the mid-1970s, I was released from prison and was finally able to go back home to my wife and son. I was truly grateful for the Lord's deliverance, but my newfound freedom did not last long. My name was still on the government's list of antirevolutionaries, so I could be arrested on even the slightest whim. As bad as things were in China overall, they were even worse for those labeled by the government as troublemakers, because we were blamed for everything. According to government officials, none of the nation's problems were due to their own policies; the blame rested solely on the antirevolutionaries. And, according to the government, I was an enemy of both the state and the people.

On January 18, 1976, I was taken by the police to stand before the people in Guaihe Village, the town in which I had grown up. Hundreds of people showed up to this public trial, in which I was made a spectacle for all to see. I stood in front of Judge Taifeng Li as he announced my crimes. He read aloud that I was an antirevolutionary clothed in religious superstition, and he ordered me to serve another seven years in prison.

Many people started handing me money, and some even gave me clothing. It was as if they were saying good-bye to me forever.

My heart sank as I stood before the judge and heard his sentence. At first, it was almost too much to bear. Another seven years in prison meant that I would not see my son grow up during his most formative years. Furthermore, given China's lack of food, it was very possible that he might not make it through those seven years. And, considering the things I had already experienced in prison, there was no guarantee that I would survive to see him again.

After the verdict was pronounced, there was much commotion in the crowd because my family members and fellow believers began weeping and wailing. The unbelievers just watched in confusion as the number of people crying out grew until their cries became a roaring lament that seemed to reach to the heavens. Many people started handing me money, and some even gave me clothing. It was as if they were saying good-bye to me forever. Many people believed that they were looking at a walking dead man.

Again, the sentence seemed too hard for me to accept, but knowing that I could easily have been executed, as so many others before me had been, I recognized that the court had actually shown me mercy. "You have twenty minutes," the officer of the court told me sternly as he motioned to the people waiting to talk to me. I nodded and turned to those who were reaching out for my hand. The believers immediately began to pray for me, and they gave me many words of encouragement; I desperately needed both their prayers and their encouragement. I knew that seven days could feel like forever in a Chinese prison, let alone seven long years.

After twenty minutes, I was led to a van, and a police officer pushed me inside while another officer pushed the crowd back as the door was shut behind me. We drove to a small town called Zhaohe. To my surprise, hundreds of people had gathered to wait for my arrival there and were now outside the van, weeping. I could hear them calling my name. At first, I didn't understand what they were doing, but then it dawned on me that my name and my offense had been broadcast over the radio. On the same day that I had been arrested and sentenced to seven years in prison, the government had announced my judgment to the public and openly accused me of various crimes.

The crowds had begun to circle the van even before we stopped moving. There was just one circle of people at first, but then another circle formed around that one. As the van moved, the people would also move without breaking the circles. Whenever the van slowed down, even more layers of people would come to surround it.

When the van finally stopped, two officers jumped out from the front seat. One of them grabbed a wooden plank. As they pulled me out of the vehicle, they put a rope around my neck, which was attached to the wooden plank. This piece of wood was about two feet long and one foot high, and there were big black letters painted on it that read, "Zhang Rongliang— Religious Antirevolutionary."

"Don't stop!" the officer yelled back at me as he prodded me in the direction of the prison. "Get back!" he shouted at the mob growing around us.

As they led me to my new home, I could not help but be humbled by the response of the believers who had put their lives and safety on the line to show me their support. I never knew there were so many believers praying for me. That night in prison, I wrote the following:

> The Lord has accepted my request that I might soon leave this world and be united with Him. I am imprisoned on earth, but it has all taken place by the Lord's love.
>
> My fellow believers, I will never forget you and all of the unspoken words that your tears shared with me. Do not keep on crying for me, because I do not have any fear regarding my life.

I understand that I am considered to be a disgrace to my ancestors, but I will remain faithful to my heavenly Father and my spiritual ancestors.

If you must keep on crying for me, please hide your faces from mine. Though I weep now, it is not because of the hunger pains or the ropes that are tightly wrapped around me. I weep because I know that our sadness will not last long. He has promised us that we will be in His kingdom forever.

My brothers, I have seen your faces and clothes soaked with tears. You were mocked and insulted, but you ignored their comments. After all, how could they comprehend the kind of love that runs deeper than that of siblings?

Believe that one day we will be united with Jesus, and that day will be full of joy! Before long, the earthly church will reap the harvest, and all the earth will shake and shout for joy! Nations will come before Him and declare that Jesus saves, and we will be free forever.

The love of those dear believers was like a wave of refreshing water; it not only helped to ease my pain but also seemed big enough to drown all the pain of China.

Once I was placed in my cell, the news came to me that my spiritual mother, Guizhen Jia, was in the women's prison next to mine. I breathed a sigh of relief, knowing that she was right next door. Again, there was something very selfish in finding comfort in knowing that my spiritual mother was so near, but I knew that her calming presence would give me strength. I thanked God for her.

That all changed on the morning of January 23. Shortly after the wake-up call, I learned that I would be transferred to another prison. I was still in the process of waking up, so the thought had to take a moment to sink in. As I pondered on it, I suddenly realized what it meant. I would not be able to meet with Guizhen Jia. I felt panicked, but I prayed that God would allow me a chance to tell her the news. Otherwise, she would not know that I had left or where I was going. There was a burning fire inside of me, urging me to find a way to tell her. I tried to find someone to pass the message on to her for me, but it was too early in the day. All the people I might have contact with throughout the day were not accessible before 7:00 a.m.

I sat near the barred door in my cell and looked down the hall as far as I could see, longing to discover a way to escape reality for just a moment to tell Guizhen that I would be leaving and that I needed her prayers. Right before seven o'clock, I heard the soldiers coming down the corridor. Their guns rattled as their feet marched over the dust-covered concrete floor. As they approached, I saw that they were carrying electric batons. My body jolted just at the sight of those rods. I was far too familiar with what they can do to human flesh.

The love of those dear believers was like a wave of refreshing water; it seemed big enough to drown all the pain of China.

At that moment, as I was sitting near the doorway, I saw a gate beyond the soldiers that led to the women's prison. The gate hadn't been secured; it was somewhat open. I slowly stood up and focused my gaze on that opening. I didn't have a plan, but I tried to come up with one fast.

Everything seemed to move in slow motion. One of the guards moved his rifle to his back hip, letting the sling swing on his shoulder. He reached down with his key and began to open the door to my cell. None of the other prisoners paid any attention to what I was doing. They didn't know that I had anything planned, and honestly, I didn't realize it, either.

I waited by the door and listened for the latch to unlock. As soon as I saw that the door was ajar, I shoved it open with all my might, knocking one of the guards back. Before the other guard had a chance to react, I thrust him out of the way.

I ran for the opening with reckless abandon. In Chinese prisons, the guards are authorized to shoot on sight. I knew that I could be shot at any time, but my adrenaline was overriding all reason. The women's prison was right in front of me and rapidly getting closer. My legs were carrying me faster than they ever had before. I had energy reserves that surprised me, and my legs seemed full of power.

As I got close to the women's prison, I yelled out, "Aunt Gui! Aunt Gui! I am being sent to another prison today. Let's pray for each other. Guizhen! I am being transferred to another prison today. Let's pray for each other."

Suddenly, all the energy was sucked out of my body by volts of electricity flowing through me. A baton placed on my neck sent the voltage all the way down to my feet in an instant. My body went limp, and I fell headfirst into the ground. The current was so powerful that I was not even able to put my hands out in front of me to break the fall. The sensation of being tackled by several guards immediately brought me back to reality—I was in prison.

Strangely, I didn't feel any pain. While lying on the ground, completely motionless, I felt a great deal of satisfaction. I was glad that I had taken the chance. Once the guards began to get up, I could feel a tug on my legs. They dragged me across the yard back into the prison. I tried to use my hands to protect my face from being dragged on the ground, but it was no use because the guards were moving too quickly.

When we reached the concrete prison floor, the corners of the front step ripped into my upper side and chest, and my chin bounced off the threshold. There was no use in protesting; it would only have wasted energy and fallen on deaf ears.

"You are going to pay for that little stunt, Zhang," said the commanding officer. "Get him up here and take off his jacket." They dragged me into the prison yard. One of the guards sat me up to take off my jacket, then shoved me back down. My head hit the ground with a loud thud. When I heard the sound of a leather whip cracking in the air, I winced, knowing full well what was coming. I rolled over to protect my face as the first lash came down on my back. There was silence in the prison yard as the whipping began. I couldn't see anyone, but I could feel that everyone's eyes were on me.

No one at the prison had had time to get to know me, so none of them knew what was happening. Over and over, the guard hit me with the whip, each strike cutting further into the flesh on my back. The long leather cord would sometimes wrap around my side and rip open the skin on its way back up.

I should have been in great pain and begging for mercy, but I wasn't. I was filled with unexplainable joy because I knew that my spiritual mother was aware that I was being moved and that she would be praying for me every day and night. That thought instantly brought comfort to me.

When they were finished whipping me, I continued lying on the ground. I tried to push myself up, but my skin was too raw. It didn't want to extend enough for me to arch out to stand up. I glanced at my shirt and saw that I was covered in my own blood. It wasn't the first time I had been beaten to a bloody pulp, nor would it be the last.

14

Uncle Feng

I was driven to a farm in the town of Xihua, Henan Province. The Xihua prison was a labor camp that covered sixty-four square kilometers, or almost twenty-five square miles, of farmland. The camp had been established in 1962, right after Mao began to send prisoners to such places for reeducation. Xihua was a prison that many people walked into but few walked out of.

I was only twenty-five years old, but I felt like an old man. All of my joints ached. After the whipping, I had to tilt my body in such a way that the clothing would not stick to my open wounds. I was shown to my cell, but I could hardly move. I could see the eyes of the other prisoners measuring me up as they did with every newcomer. I'm sure that everyone's first impression of me was that I was a slow, weak young man.

In the view of the prison guards and even the prisoners, everyone who entered the prison was either a potential benefit or a potential burden. In general, there were two types of new prisoners: those who were young and strong and therefore able to lighten the workload in the field, and those who were old and feeble with soft hands and thus unable to help much. A new prisoner in the second group merely added to the burden by being just another mouth to feed.

Soon after I arrived, I started hearing rumors from around the camp. I quickly learned that we were given only thirty-six kilograms, or about eighty pounds, of rice per month; consequently, starvation was a serious issue. There was also no doctor in the camp, so getting sick wasn't an option. On top of these things, we had to do backbreaking labor every day. This was what life was like for every prisoner at Xihua Labor Camp.

The prison guard's wife was a sister in the Lord. For the next six months, she sent me food and medicine.

The lack of proper nutrition combined with the strenuous work schedule took its toll on me, and I soon fell sick. My illness was not serious, but it lingered for three months due to malnutrition and lack of medical care. I imagined that my health would continue to deteriorate until I was dead and buried. After I had been ill for three months, I was worthless as a field hand. I was not able to push a plow or even pull weeds. All of the energy had been sapped from my body. In the midst of such utter weakness, the Lord demonstrated His love and mercy toward me in the most amazing way.

One day, a guard came to me and said softly and with unusual kindness, "Zhang Rongliang, my wife heard about your illness and had me buy you this medicine. It's our secret, so don't tell others." He placed a small package in my hands that he had kept hidden until then. When I opened it, I saw that he had given me medicine and extra food. I could not believe my eyes! The Lord had been so gracious to me in my moment of great need. Some of King David's words in the Psalms came to mind; God was indeed my help and the *"God of my salvation"* (Psalm 27:9).

I later found out that the prison guard's wife was a sister in the Lord. For the next six months, she sent me food and medicine; this assistance not only helped me to recover from the illness but also kept me healthy afterward. Her husband risked his life to sneak the items into the prison and hand them to me. The Lord had truly prepared a table for me in the midst of my enemies! (See Psalm 23:5.) Even though I had assumed that I would die, the Lord showed me that He was not yet ready to take me from this earth, and He continued to provide for me.

One day, I got word that Feng Jianguo, known as "Uncle Feng," was going to be transferred to Xihua camp. I was overjoyed at the news. Uncle Feng was a powerful preacher who had founded the underground house church network China Gospel Fellowship.

China Gospel Fellowship, referred to simply as "Tanghe" by the majority of its members, is one of the most well-known underground house church networks. Containing millions of believers, this group has more members than the entire population of many European countries! Like most underground networks in China, the Tanghe fellowship is named after the county in which it began, Tanghe County in Henan Province. Uncle Feng was a dynamic preacher in Tanghe County during the 1970s but was considered to be an enemy of the Chinese Communist Party. I had heard about his powerful ministry, and apparently the government had, as well.

Uncle Feng had not set out with some ambitious plan to start a huge fellowship but was simply faithful in preaching the gospel. His being forced to travel from one village to the next with the police hot on his tail resulted in churches being planted throughout a large section of China. Whenever the police would arrest members from those churches, they would simply say, "We are from Tanghe Church." The persecution led to the establishment of a mighty army of fearless soldiers for Christ.

Uncle Feng was branded as an antirevolutionary and marked by the Party, which would not rest until he was apprehended. It was not long before the law caught up with him. After he was arrested, Uncle Feng was interrogated, beaten, and sent to the jail in Nanyang. He stayed there for about a year before he was sent to our labor camp in Xihua.

Xihua Labor Camp had been divided into various sectors with different farms, so I knew it might be impossible for me to find him. But I had heard about all the amazing things that God had done through his life, and I was sure that I would greatly benefit from his fellowship given the opportunity. I had no idea that some brothers in Nanyang had already told him that I was in Xihua and that all of them were praying that he would meet me.

The part of the camp I had been assigned to was quite near the main farm, so I could hear what was going on at the main gate and in the prison yard. One day, soon after I heard the news about Uncle Feng, buses came in through the camp gates. The buses kept coming and coming until their contents—six hundred new prisoners—flooded the prison yard. The guards moved the new arrivals into more manageable groups, and then each group was divided into sections. Guards for each of the sections led the prisoners to their assigned areas.

Out of six hundred new prisoners, God had sovereignly arranged for the one I needed to meet the most to be placed in my own cell!

One of the guards yelled for me to come over and bring one of the last groups of newcomers to my cell block. As I walked over there, I heard the footsteps of those being led to my section. "Line up!" the guard yelled at the group. I could tell that everyone was getting tired. The guards wanted to get to bed as much as we did. "When I point to you," the guard told the inmates, "step forward and sound off with your name."

Then he pointed to one of the new prisoners and said, "You." The prisoner stepped forward and yelled out, "Prisoner Feng Jianguo, an antirevolutionary criminal!" Immediately, I looked over at him. He was tired, but I could see the joy of the Lord on his face. His cheeks were sunken from malnutrition, and his hair was disheveled. I could tell that he needed rest and restoration, and I was going to do my best to provide it.

"Zhang! Find this prisoner a bed."

"Yes, sir!" I rushed over, took Uncle Feng's luggage from him, and carried it back toward my cell. Out of six hundred new prisoners placed in a camp filled with hundreds of others, God had sovereignly arranged for the one I needed to meet the most to be placed in my own cell! God had heard the prayers of His children once again.

After we arrived at the cell and I had shown him his bed, we looked around to see who was watching. We were allowed to talk because I was helping a new prisoner, and I was expected to introduce him to the camp procedures. When I saw that no one was looking, I grabbed Uncle Feng's hands, and we immediately began to pray together. It was such a precious time, and the Spirit of the Lord moved mightily. I started to cry out uncontrollably, and my tears carved channels through the dirt on my face.

Feng began to cry, as well. We just stood there holding on to each other and weeping before the Lord. We didn't know what the next day would bring or if we would live to see the outside of the prison walls, but that night we did know that the Lord was with us. He smiled upon us, and it was like the warm sun shining on our faces.

Early days: Zhang Rongliang with his son.

Teaching in a secret, hand-dug cave in Henan Province where thousands of Chinese pastors were trained.

Four giants of the faith in China's house church(from left): Brother Yun, Enoch Wang, Peter Xu, and Zhang Rongliang

Preaching at a conference.

Zhang pictured during his most recent prison term.

Zhang in Fangcheng.

15

"The Lord Hears the Prisoners' Groans"

No heat and a lack of warm clothes made for a very difficult winter at Xihua Labor Camp. But winter came and went, and soon the summer of 1977 arrived. I was thankful that the Lord had kept me alive. I was getting used to life at the camp, although it was not becoming any easier.

I needed a private place where I could be alone with God, where I could study and meditate on the Word without being interrupted or caught by the guards, so I asked the Lord to provide it. As ridiculous as it sounds given my situation, I wanted a place where I could sing hymns without anyone else hearing me.

One night, I had a dream in which a policeman came and took me just outside a room that was full of pigs. I couldn't go inside the room because the door was locked, and although the policeman motioned for me to go in, I didn't have the key to unlock the door. In the dream, I desperately wanted to go in, but it was impossible without the key. I kept looking down at my hand, but it was always empty.

It had been such a powerful dream that it was still vivid in my mind when I woke up. I kept thinking about how there was nothing I could do because I didn't have a key. Suddenly, this thought came to me: *I can't open the door because I don't have a key. Prayer is the key. If I want to open that door, I need to pray.*

I rolled over onto my knees and began to pray before the Lord for a room by myself. "Lord, please forgive me. I have not been on my knees in front of You like this for three and a half years! I cry out to You and ask You to forgive my ignorance. Hear my prayer, O Lord, and allow me to have a private place where I can pray and commune with You. I want nothing more, Father."

God had answered my prayer by moving me to a pigpen! I had all the privacy I wanted and more freedom than I ever could have dreamed of.

Later that evening, Brother Liu, one of the believers who lived in town, snuck into camp to visit me after everyone was sound asleep. "Zhang," he said, "the Lord spoke to me today and told me that tomorrow you will be living out with the pigs. The Lord told me that your prayer will be answered, but you are to keep it a secret until the hour in which it comes to pass. Do not share these words with anyone else."

I could not believe my ears! I was experiencing firsthand that profound truth in God's Word that says that the Lord *"hear[s] the groans of the prisoners"* (Psalm 102:20). The Lord is the God who listens to prayers.

The next morning, a guard came to my room, took me to the area where the pigs were fed, and told me that this would be my new residence and my new job. God had answered my prayer by moving me to a pigpen! I loved sleeping in that pigpen; it was like heaven on earth. I had all the privacy I wanted and more freedom than I ever could have dreamed of.

I was so far from the rest of the camp that most guards didn't bother to venture out to check on me as often as they had previously. The nights were virtually free from any hassle from the guards. Since I wasn't noisy, they left me alone. Coming out and overseeing my work would have added to their own workload, and I was not deemed worth the trouble.

I spent my days praising the Lord as I worked. In the beginning, I did so quietly; but after a few days, it was clear that no one would bother me, least of all the pigs. When evening settled in, I began to roam around outside. I would pray and sing to God with the starry skies overhead. I knew that the guards never came to check on me in the evening, and one night, as I was praying, I thought about leaving the prison. An idea rushed over me like a tidal wave, and once it was in my head, I was not able to shake it. The field that I worked in was not monitored because the whole area was too large. I realized that nobody would ever know if I were just to keep walking past the outer border of the camp and go into the nearby villages to preach the gospel late at night. My desire to worship with other brothers and sisters was greater than my instinct for self-preservation, so one night, I snuck out and headed to the nearest village.

Once I got close to the village, I stepped lightly on the areas where there was no grass. I didn't want to alert the dogs guarding the community. The sound of the crickets was almost loud enough to cover any movement I made. The only thing that was louder than the crickets was my heartbeat. I was almost certain that my heart was pounding loud enough to be heard down the street. It felt like it was going to burst out of my chest.

I was not very familiar with the village, but I remembered enough to get around. I was able to meet with Brother Liu, and we became partners in ministry. He loaned me his bicycle—a luxury in those days of nationwide poverty—so I could go back and forth to the camp more quickly. The opportunity to be ministered to and to minister to other Christians through preaching was a dream come true for me. Night after night, I would leave the prison camp and use Liu's bicycle to travel to the neighboring villages, preaching the gospel and exhorting the churches everywhere I went. Today, Brother Liu still works as a leader in his local church, faithfully feeding the sheep of the whole town of Xihua. Wonders and miracles follow him wherever he goes.

After a while, I took off my prison uniform and began to wear my own clothes, even in the camp. I wore the standard blue outfit made popular by Mao Zedong. The prison budget was not large enough to supply everyone in the prison with the needed clothing, anyway, so it was not a big deal. The prison guards did not mind that I wore my own clothes, and my new attire made it much easier for me to go back and forth to the villages without attracting suspicion.

I developed a routine of sneaking out of the prison every evening and getting back before dawn. Every time I returned to the prison, I would begin the day by getting everything cleaned up from the evening before. I would clean the floors and the pigsties and get the pens ready for feeding the animals. I would then prepare the feed by mixing corn and wheat.

I never would have been able to preach in certain villages if I had not been imprisoned nearby.

I fed the pigs about three times a day. If I did not have enough grain, I would go out into the yard and gather clumps of grass to supplement the deficiency. This meant that I could use the pigs as an excuse if I ever got caught sneaking out of the prison camp. The fact that I needed to venture beyond the confines of the camp at times just to find food for the pigs was a perfect and truthful alibi.

Over time, I developed a close relationship with the pigs and always tried to bring them something to eat from my late-night excursions. It got to the point where I could walk away from the pigpen even during the day, and the guards would not be concerned because they would see me returning hours later with large piles of grass in my arms for the pigs. If any of the pigs got sick, I would place my hands on it and pray for its health. I knew that God cared about the pigs and that He cared about their sicknesses. As long as the pigs were happy, healthy, and fat, the prison guards were happy.

I was greatly tempted to simply run away once I had already escaped to the villages, but I continually reminded myself that God had given me a special opportunity that I might not have if I was a fugitive on the run. Things had started to look up for me. I felt free. I was able to preach the gospel, train disciples, plant churches, and build up those churches in over five different villages near the labor camp.

I never would have been able to preach in those villages if I had not been imprisoned nearby. Life was not easy at Xihua, but I was thankful for it. As long as I was back by sunrise and the pigs were properly cared for, everything continued as normal at the camp and I was able to minister in the villages at night. Despite the tiring schedule, it was an almost perfect situation—almost. Getting too comfortable with our circumstances is always dangerous and can lead to physical and spiritual laziness. I had become too comfortable in my pigpen. I was not being as careful as I would have if I had been with the general population in the camp.

Because I was free to visit the villages at night, I had been able to procure a Bible, which I took back with me to the labor camp. In those days, anywhere in China, a Bible was a very precious item. It was even more precious in prison, where such antirevolutionary material was strictly forbidden. While I was working in the fields during the day, I would hide my Bible in a pile of pig food so no one would be able to find it. I was very careful to make sure that the area where I hid my Bible did not have enough moisture to destroy those precious pages.

At first, I was very cautious with my Bible and made sure it was hidden in the most concealed place possible; but over time, I gradually started becoming more relaxed. Then, in the autumn of 1978, I was working in the field when I heard everyone called together. I stopped and looked around, and I could tell that there was a great deal of anxiety in the air. The guards were moving to and fro with purpose and intensity. It was clear that something was happening, but I was not sure what.

I soon found out: It was a raid! The guards were making an unannounced inspection of all our living quarters to look for contraband. I immediately thought of my room in the pigpen, knowing that they would likely find a gold mine of illegal materials there.

I headed for my room in hopes that I could make it there before the guards did, but as I neared the pigpen, I saw that I was too late. The guards were there, and they had already gone through all my things. I kept my distance so that I could observe without being seen. From their reaction, I could tell that they had found everything.

My heart started to thump louder and faster. There really was no set punishment for having a Bible because nobody ever had one. But I knew that the guards had amazingly creative imaginations and could find the cruelest ways to make me pay for having that Bible.

Rumors began to go through the prison that the guards had found my Bible, as well as several documents mentioning other Christians in the prison and some of the work that I had been doing in the villages. Right away, I made my way around to tell the other believers that my documents had been compromised and that they could deny knowing anything about my activities. My brothers immediately began to pray about the situation.

At first, I was really nervous and didn't have any plan for how to rectify the situation. "O Lord," I prayed. "You told us that if we ask, we shall receive. In Your name, I am requesting that this storm be immediately calmed. I am asking You to help me get my Bible back."

As soon as the words came out of my mouth, I had an idea. It was not a good idea, but I thought that it might just be crazy enough to work. I stopped being afraid and trusted in the Lord. I walked toward the main office of the prison and went right into the building to see the officer in charge, whose name was Liu.

"Officer Liu, sir."

Liu looked up from his desk. He was startled to see me standing in front of him.

"Zhang? What do you want?" he asked.

"Today, some of your men took my book and six pages of documents from my quarters. I would like them back now."

Liu hesitated for a moment before saying, "Well, um...." I could tell that he was searching for a response but didn't have one. There was actually a faint expression of fear on his face.

I repeated, "Your guys came into my room and confiscated my belongings, and now I need them to be returned to my possession."

Officer Liu got up from where he was sitting and went to search for my Bible and church documents. Once he found them, he gave them back to me. Problem solved.

In hindsight, I was really out of my mind to do that, but I praise God for answering my prayer. That moment was one of the most amazing answers to prayer I have ever experienced.

16

The Chinese "Purim"

A tremendous harvest of new believers came to Lord between 1977 and 1979. Chairman Mao Zedong had died in September 1976, and he had been replaced for a very short time by the "Gang of Four," a group of Communist officials led by Mao's wife, Jiang Qing. In the end, Jiang Qing and her three political partners took the blame for all the failed policies that had led to widespread suffering throughout the nation during the Cultural Revolution. They were tried in court, and Jiang Qing received the death sentence, which was later commuted to life in prison. She eventually hanged herself in a bathroom, leaving a note that read, "Chairman, your student and fighter is coming to see you!"

Jiang Qing's death marked a shift in the persecution of Christians. She had been one of the fiercest opponents of Christianity and had been committed to stomping it out entirely. She had even been noted as saying to a foreign reporter that Christianity in China no longer existed, that it "has been confined to the history section of the museum. It is dead and buried." Now she is the one who is dead and buried, and the name of Jesus is being proclaimed all across China, to the praise of His glorious grace!

The whole situation reminded me of the Jewish celebration of Purim, which commemorates the events recorded in the book of Esther. Just as the Jews had been freed from Haman's evil plan for their annihilation, God had freed the Christians in China from their fiercest earthly adversary. Like Esther, thousands of Christians across China had prayed and fasted for the protection of God's people. In 1976, Chinese Christians had felt as if they were in the jaws of death, about to be chomped to bits, but God had heard the prayers of His children, and He had suddenly rescued them. Upon hearing about the death of Jiang Qing, people all over China shouted with joy in the streets. I will forever remember those days as China's "Purim."

In 1976, Chinese Christians had felt as if they were in the jaws of death, but God had heard the prayers of His children, and He had suddenly rescued them.

With Chairman Mao dead, the nation of China was ready to close one of the darkest chapters in its history. Mao's successor, Deng Xiaoping, was ready to take the country in a new direction. Deng Xiaoping successfully began to marginalize and punish the extreme leftists; and under his new policies, the landowners, educated professionals, and former businessmen were pulled out from the shadows.

The growing number of Christians had an unforeseen side effect: More people were going to visit fellow believers who were serving prison sentences for the sake of the gospel. It was a major turn of events. Sometimes, it seemed as if there was an endless stream of visitors making their way to the prison to see me. Having visitors come to spend time with me was very humbling, as well as encouraging. My strength was renewed by the words they shared with me, and many of them also expressed great admiration for my privilege of being a prisoner for the sake of the Lord.

One of the visitors from Fangcheng County church asked me what I thought about the subject of suffering. I pondered that question for hours, and it will be hard for those who have not experienced what I have been through to understand my feelings about it. Christians are a peculiar people, and I consider myself to be a proud member among them. Suffering has walked with me since I began my journey with the Lord, but it is not the only experience I have had. My suffering has been peppered with intense moments of joy and bliss.

After the visitor left and I found myself alone with my thoughts, I decided to write down in my journal my understanding of the meaning of suffering. This is what I wrote:

Suffering challenges so many people in the world.
Without suffering, how is it possible to taste the depths of the
    goodness of the Lord?
After tasting, how can one be obsessed with worldly desires?
O Suffering, I used to flee from you.
But today the Lord has commanded me to endure all that you
    have for me.
O Suffering, did the apostles not welcome you?
Suffering invites the seekers to go along with him.
He calls out to me and says, "Come and shake my hand."
O Suffering, let me embrace you.
It tastes good that I was with you in the Lord.
O Suffering, how many disciples have you fed?
Without you, life has lost its struggle.
I ask you to visit me.
Let me taste only a bit of the sweetness that you give.
O Suffering, you make the moments with my Lord so much better.
You are the oxygen of the saints.
Without you, they would have stopped breathing.
You are so close to me.
O Suffering, let us walk arm in arm together.

Xihua Prison
March 1978

Things were changing rapidly in 1978 following the political upheaval, and our labor camp was not immune to these shifts. Most of the prisoners in our camp had been labeled as antirevolutionaries, and it was time to start releasing them. Under the new leader, Deng Xiaoping, the antirevolutionaries were not considered as bad as they had been under the hard-line rule of Mao Zedong. Soon, prison officials began to release inmates and let them to go home. They were setting free three or four people every day. They wanted to release me and let me go home, too, but first they needed to hear me say that I had been "rehabilitated."

One of the leaders cornered me and got in my face, saying, "Religion is a myth. It is a fairy tale used by imperialists to invade nations. It is like a chain, keeping those in poverty enslaved to the imperialists." I watched his lips move, and I listened as he accented each word. I could feel a fire rising up inside me. I was getting angrier by the second. He continued to rant, but I couldn't hear him any longer. I felt that he was ignorant and clueless to the power that our mighty God held in His hand. He was awakening a roaring lion inside of me, and I barked back, "Know this! I cannot be rehabilitated from truth to ignorance."

I walked away without requesting permission to leave. I knew that this had been my chance to leave the prison. The guard was actually trying to get me to acknowledge his words as truth so that I could return home, so I had basically blown any chance of leaving the labor camp. However, in my mind, nothing about my experience in prison had changed. The conditions remained the same. If people denied Jesus, they would be set free. I had faced this situation so many times in the past. I hadn't denied my Lord before, and I didn't know what led them to believe that I would do so now. The authorities seemed to have great faith in their abilities to make me abandon Christ. They were convinced they could change me, and in that way they demonstrated levels of faith that I have not seen in most Christians.

I remained in the labor camp for the next two years while the guards worked overtime to get me expedited from prison. After a while, a government official was sent to give me personal classes. He tried to teach me that Jesus was actually not a very good person at all, but the official's efforts were all for naught. I told them that I would benefit more by spending time with the pigs. I wasn't being difficult; I was just being honest.

On January 10, 1980, everyone was called out for the daily roll call. It was cold and dark, and nothing seemed different about that cold morning than any other morning. I stood in the formation shivering and ready to get back to feeding the pigs.

"Zhang Rongliang!" a guard yelled. I paused for a moment. It is never a good thing to hear your name barked out in a labor camp.

"Here!" I responded.

"Zhang, pack your things. You are going home today. You're out of here."

Just like that, after having served three years of a seven-year sentence, I was being released from Xihua Labor Camp. That day, before my release, I paced around the area where I had stayed for those long years. It was actually hard for me to say good-bye to a place in which I had spent so many sweet hours with the Lord. Then I stood in my room and prayed my last prayer in that prison. "Lord, how many years You have spent with me in this jail! I still remember how You helped me through it all and how I was comforted by other brothers. You have taught me so many lessons within these walls. Lord, please accept my prayer. When my son is able to do house chores, send me back!"

Years had passed since I had last seen my family. I dearly missed my parents, my wife, and my son, but I knew that the first thing I wanted to do when I was released was to visit a church and thank God for all He had done for me.

17

Never Safe to Stay Still

Freedom from prison has a sweet flavor that the common citizen will never know. As I prepared to walk out the gates of Xihua Labor Camp, I understood that I was still 250 kilometers, or more than 150 miles, from home—but home felt much closer to me than it had the day before. It was liberating to leave the prison without anyone directing me where to go or when to stop. I filled my lungs with air, and it felt so fresh to me because I was breathing it as a free man. Everything seemed so alive.

Upon my release, I had been given a little money with which to travel home. From Tian Kou Village, I walked to the local bus station in Zhoukou City. As I waited for the bus, I tried to act as naturally as I could. After the bus arrived, coming to a screeching halt, I climbed on board and found a seat by a window. I wanted to sit where I could watch the road go by as I thought about seeing my wife and son again.

In the deepest recesses of my mind, I had a quiet love for my wife that had been lying dormant for quite some time. I never forgot her, but regularly thinking about her in prison would have driven me to insanity. She was the one with whom I wanted to share everything, but it was not easy to put into words what she could not fully understand until she herself had accepted Christ as her Lord and Savior.

In 1978, she had walked a lonely path, but it was during those dark days that she had called out to Christ for the first time and repented of all of her sins. I find it mysteriously strange how things worked out. I had shared the gospel with her on many occasions. Through my talks with her, I had drained myself of all my knowledge and words about the Word of God. I had left no stone unturned in looking for ways to lead her to Christ. Nothing I had done had worked, but when the time was right, without my even being present, our sovereign God had brought her to Himself.

During the years I spent in prison, many sisters and brothers from the church had visited my wife and helped to meet her material needs. Even so, those were tough times for her. In 1978, during the most joyous time of the year in China, the Chinese New Year, everyone in our hometown was preparing for the festival. My wife longingly watched others as they got together with their families and prepared food. She had absolutely nothing. Our son cried often during those days because he was so hungry, and there was no food to give him. My wife didn't have money for salt or oil to prepare anything, even if she could find something to cook. Thus, all around her, people were engaged in celebration; but in our home, my wife could only mourn the impending death she knew would arrive soon if she didn't find a way to get food.

Although my wife was desperate, she had not spoken about her needs to anyone. She knew that it would not make a difference, anyway. Everyone else was also buried knee-deep in poverty, so they couldn't help much. However, God met her need by reaching out and touching the heart of a dear brother named Shuqian Zheng, who lived about sixty-four kilometers, or forty miles, away. He had only sixteen renminbi, which, at that time, was the equivalent of a little less than two American dollars. God told him to travel to our village and give half his money to my wife. The dear brother obediently followed the leading of the Holy Spirit, left his home, and walked all that way in the cold to give her the money.

My wife heard a knock on the door, and when she answered it, Brother Zheng was standing there. On that day, after she found out why he had come, she could no longer rationalize why she had not yet accepted Christ as her Lord and Savior. As she stood in our broken wooden doorway, staring into the wild eyes of a man who was convinced that God had told him to walk forty miles to her house to give her money, she lost her composure. Her legs gave out underneath her, and she collapsed to the floor. Through the dust that rested on her cheeks, tears flowed down and made puddles on the dirt floor. The God who had been so alien to her for so long had finally become her Father—a loving Father who looks out for His children and cares intimately for their individual needs.

I had learned about her conversion while I was in prison. Two years later, I found myself sitting on a bus, trying to make my way to her as fast as I could. Chinese are different from people of other cultures, and those differences are sometimes highlighted in our application of the Scriptures. As I rode that bus, a verse from Luke came to mind, and the words rolled off my tongue: *"If anyone comes to Me and does not hate his own father and mother, wife and children, brothers and sisters—yes, and even his own life—he cannot be My disciple"* (Luke 14:26 HCSB).

> The God who had been so alien to her for so long had finally become her Father—a loving Father who looks out for His children and cares intimately for their individual needs.

This verse seems to have an air of cold shrillness; but through spiritual insight and mature character, we are led to understand that Jesus' words refer to the most sacrificial love known to mankind. The verse is not saying that we are to hate our closest relatives, because the Bible clearly tells us to love, not hate. Rather, it is telling us that we must put Christ first in our lives, above all others. In that moment, as I rode the bus, this Scripture spoke to me specifically, giving me direction as clearly as a road construction sign with bold letters and flashing lights, guiding motorists about what lane to drive in and what detour to take.

It was true that I needed to see my wife and my son, whom I had not laid eyes on since he was only six months old; but God was telling me to visit some other believers first. I was not even dimly aware of His purpose, but I followed His instructions anyway. I soon found myself at the house of Sister Jiang. Upon my arrival, there was a festive feeling in the air, and

Sister Chen immediately cooked up a meal for everyone; she prepared a seemingly inexhaustible variety of food. Sister Chen reminded me of the poor woman described in the Bible who gave all that she had to honor God. (See Luke 21:1–4.) Friends both old and new came from all over the village to join us. Then, without any introduction or ceremony, I impulsively stood up and began to preach. We all enjoyed the food, but it was the Lord who had brought us together, and the Lord had given me a message to share with His people.

After I left that night, I traveled to three more households in different towns before finally reaching my own home fifteen days later. I had been out of prison for more than two weeks, but I hadn't yet seen my family, and my heart ached to see my wife and son. I had imagined over and over in my mind what our reunion would be like. When I arrived, I ran over and scooped up my son in my arms. He had already grown to be such a big boy. Tears were streaming down my wife's face. Time stood still as we rejoiced with one another.

My wife prepared a homecoming meal for me that took me back to better days. Friends and family members trickled into our small home one by one. Each of them kicked up more and more dust at the door as they entered! The number of new believers in our village had surpassed anything that I had thought possible. Men came to my home to welcome me who had previously made public pronouncements of atheism. Those who had mocked me, persecuted me, and hurled insults at my wife and me were now rejoicing with me in the name of Jesus. I was speechless. I was no longer a lone Christian in a sea of sinners but part of a steadily growing body of believers. The fear of persecution, arrest, and death did not dissuade them.

Poverty and persecution had not killed the church in China. Instead, the church was growing into a beautiful and pure bride of Christ. There is a traditional Chinese saying, passed down to us from our ancestors, that says, "You die so that I can live." It is used to describe your enemy in battle. You don't want to die, so you must take the life of your enemy. You don't give your life for your cause; you make the enemy give his life, and then you can eliminate the threat. This idea has been passed down from generation to generation for thousands of years in China; but two thousand years ago

Jesus gave us a new life and a new way to live. Now Christians in China must claim, "I must die so that Jesus can live in me." We must decrease in every way so that He might increase. (See John 3:30.)

After I returned home, I heard talk about one of my neighbors, Wubo Tian. Even though he was known to be a man of great integrity, he was also known to have a bad temper and to hold grudges—and he deeply hated me and my family. When I was commander of the area for the Communist Party, a raid had been carried out on Wubo's home because he kept traditional religious idols there. Wubo did not react kindly to having his home raided, and he was treated harshly. He assumed that I was the initiator of the raid because of my high position, but I was not even aware of it.

During the time when I was imprisoned, Wubo had gone around celebrating. He had loudly shouted to everyone who would listen that I was an evil man and deserved to be in prison. When I worked on the mountain as a member of the Black Five, he was one of those who would come to see me on a regular basis in order to hurl insults at me. So, when I returned home from prison, Wubo automatically assumed that I would seek revenge against him. In fact, he was afraid that I would hire someone to kill him and that I might even have someone murder his entire family at night while they slept.

Poverty and persecution had not killed the church in China. Instead, the church was growing into a beautiful and pure bride of Christ.

I knew in my heart that I had to go and let Wubo know about the great God whom I serve. He saw me as his enemy, but I saw him as a family member. God had created Wubo, and He loved him; and because of God's love for him, I also loved him. It is no longer I who live but Christ who lives in me. (See Galatians 2:20.)

I bought gifts for the spring festival to give to Wubo. It was not a long walk from my home to his, only about one kilometer, or a little more than half a mile. When I arrived at his home, he answered the door. When he saw who it was, his eyes went wild with alarm. He was only twenty years older than I, but he looked famished and gaunt, which added years to him.

"Dear Wubo," I began. His family peered out from behind him, expecting the worst. "I come to you bringing these gifts," I continued as I pulled out the desserts and other treats that I had brought for him and his family. "Please accept these gifts as a token of my friendship. Please forgive me for anything that I have done to wrong you or your family." By the time I said the word "forgive," tears had already started to flow from the corners of my eyes.

The family was disarmed, and Wubo's suspicion turned to confusion. His eyes narrowed in on me as I offered the gifts to him. In an instant, his defenses were demolished by the love of Christ, and he began to weep. "Oh, please forgive me, Zhang!" he replied. "Please forgive me for what I have done to you." We embraced while his family watched in amazement.

"I need to tell you why I came here," I said, and then I told the entire family about the love of Jesus Christ. That afternoon, Wubo and his family accepted Jesus as Savior. Wubo didn't become just my friend that afternoon—he became my brother. Furthermore, Wubo's son and grandson later played a major part in the building of the church in Fangcheng.

I had learned early on as a Christian in China that it was never safe to stay still for too long. Safety came from moving often and erratically, without set patterns. I longed to stay home with my family, but a preacher in the underground house church was immobile solely if he was in a prison cell where his travels were restricted by iron bars. The only way for a pastor to work outside of prison was to be on the move, so I knew I could not stay home for long.

18

The Message Went Forth like Lightning

By March 1980, the number of young people joining our fellowship was growing beyond our capacity. After my release from prison, we decided to have a meeting for young people, and we were completely taken by surprise when more than eight hundred showed up! The energy of those young people electrified the air. The older people were excited to see that so many younger people had given their lives to Christ. It encouraged them to know that the name of Jesus would continue to be proclaimed in China long after they were gone.

We assigned brothers to position themselves on the outer edges of our large gathering so they could to alert everyone if the police showed up, and so they could delay the police from entering the meeting. As I looked around at the crowd, I knew it would be only a matter of time before the local authorities were notified. In China, people are not allowed to congregate without registering first.

When the local police heard that there were eight hundred young people rallying in our town, they put together a team of twelve fully armed soldiers under the command of a man named Wen Furong. When Furong arrived, he expected that he would be met with fear and trembling. He was ready for his small team to capitalize on their authority, break up the meeting, and detain the organizers.

I suspect that what he found was not exactly as he had imagined. The men standing around the radius of the young people would not allow the soldiers to go through. They stood shoulder to shoulder, allowing no daylight between their bodies. The young people, watching the example of the leadership, also embraced a new level of boldness and refused to disperse.

The very government that had taken away my freedom without a second thought was now backing down to a group of believers who refused to fear them.

Wen Furong was furious at such a blatant challenge to his authority. He demanded to see the owner of the property where we were meeting. When the owner presented himself, Furong yelled, "What are all these people doing at your home?" His threats and aggressive behavior did not earn him any favors from the owner of the house. With almost a bit of nonchalance, the owner simply replied, "I don't know where all these people are from, and I honestly don't know where they are going, but I invited them here when I prayed for this meeting."

Realizing that there was nothing more he could do, Furong put his finger into the air and waved for all his men to fall back and follow him off the property. A victorious cheer filled the air. It was almost like a battle cry of victory. Everyone rejoiced as they were energized by the young crowd.

Having just come out of prison, I was greatly surprised as I watched these events unfold. The very government that had taken away my freedom without a second thought was now backing down to a group of believers who refused to fear them. No violence was used. No one was hurt. We were simply standing together in unity, and it felt so exhilarating.

The number of people coming to the Lord on a daily basis continued to grow. Imagine fishing in a place where you couldn't pull your fishing line out of the water and replace it fast enough because the fish were constantly biting on the line. That is how it was in China in those days.

With the rapidly growing numbers, we were in desperate need of Bibles. As the winter closed in that year, my coworker, Elder Zhang, and I had to think of a way to get our hands on some new Bibles. The Word of God was our lifeline to salvation. Without it, there would be mass heresy on a scale that had never been seen before.

Elder Zhang and I decided that our best chance to get Bibles would be to travel to Shanghai. We had heard that Shanghai had a delivery of Bibles coming in, and if we could go there, we might be able to get our hands on a few and bring them back to our church. Our fellowship didn't have much money, but the church sent us out with enough funds to travel to Shanghai by train. Soon after Zhang and I arrived there, we found ourselves standing on the steps of Pastor Li Tianen's house, the same pastor whom I had snuck out to hear when I was working with the Black Five.

Li Tianen spent a lot of time ministering in our area of Nanyang, but his home was in Shanghai. He paid a dear price for his faith in Jesus Christ, but Shanghai was his place of retreat when he was tired and needed to rest. He also had access to more resources there than he had in Henan Province. The Shanghai Christian community was a little different from the Henan Province Christian community. Henan Province was full of backward rural communities where the pastors and laymen were common, uneducated farmers and blue-collar workers. The Shanghai Christian community came from a long, rich tradition of educated scholars who dutifully studied and dissected the Word of God under the tutelage of an army of foreign missionaries. Some of the most well-known Chinese Christian writings came out of Shanghai.

Li Tianen told us that a Bible, as well as a cassette player that had a recording of the Bible on it, were expected to arrive soon. When Elder Zhang heard that, he grew very excited and said, "Zhang, I need the recorder. I cannot read, and listening to the Word of God will be a huge blessing for me. Can you imagine? I will be able to hear the Word of God any time I want to and repeat it to others!" I couldn't help but be excited with him. "Zhang," he continued, "I think I am also going to use the Bible for our church. The people there can read the Bible to each other."

"Okay," I replied before I had a chance to fully think it through. We had traveled all the way to Shanghai, but the only things we had procured so far were one Bible and one cassette player. And they had not even arrived in Shanghai yet; we were only *hoping* to receive them.

Our one solitary Bible seemed like the equivalent of trying to use a single drop of water to raise the level of the ocean.

Zhang and I waited for ten days at Pastor Li Tianen's house. He was kind to us and gave us the best of everything. We didn't have any money to give him because we had only the equivalent of fifty American cents to last both of us for the entire ten days of waiting for the Bible. We knew that Pastor Li would not be able to feed us every day. Everyone was poor and had little to spare.

Zhang and I would leave very early in the morning and find places in town to spend the day so we wouldn't inconvenience Pastor Li. He thought that we had other meetings to attend during that time, but actually we were just making excuses. When we returned in the evening, we gave him the impression that we had already eaten so that he would not have to worry about us.

After we finally got the Bible and the cassette player in our hands, everything seemed worth it. We started back to our hometown with our new Bible, and we felt so successful! But that feeling of success quickly evaporated when we passed through a town in our county called Po River. As we talked with the local believers there, they informed us that the number of Christians in their town had already exceeded eighty thousand. Their church was not growing person by person, but village by village!

"Are there really eighty thousand believers?" I asked.

"Look in every home, on every hill, at every bridge crossing—they are all Christians now, singing and praising the Lord on every corner."

Suddenly, our one solitary Bible seemed like the equivalent of trying to use a single drop of water to raise the level of the ocean. However, not every area was experiencing the same growth that Po River was, and after hearing about the church growth in that town, I wanted to just stay there and focus my efforts where the fruit was already hanging low. However, we journeyed home.

Every Friday night, I was committed to preaching at a village that was about twelve miles from my home. One Friday night, it started to rain, and when I looked out my window, I felt a heaviness inside and a desire to stay inside. "I don't want to go tonight," I told the Lord in an almost belligerent manner. "It is raining outside, and You know that not many people will come because of the rain." I was trying to reason with the Lord, but it was not working in my favor. The prayer felt as useless as it had sounded the moment it left my lips, but I had felt obligated to voice my concern in my irrational attempt to obtain the Lord's consent to be excused.

The Lord answered me, *Be a good shepherd.* Those words echoed in my head with an undeniable, ringing truth that could not be countered by a lazy argument. Reluctantly, I put on my raincoat and walked twelve miles in the pouring rain. When I arrived, I saw that only one man had come to listen. As soon as I saw that, I felt very justified about my argument before the Lord. I almost wanted to point my finger toward the man and then look up to the Lord and say, "See!" as a pathetic attempt to extract some sort of pity or understanding from Him about the situation.

Unfortunately for my argument, the man was a good listener; he took the words that I shared with him that evening and completely gave his heart over to God. The next day, he went out and preached the Word of God, and many people came to the Lord. Then I was glad that God didn't point to all the people who had been reached through this one man and say to me, "See!" God is sovereign, and we must obey Him.

That one man inspired me. I realized that Christians were not intended to only consume God's Word; they also had a commission to share it. I called a meeting of five hundred believers whom I had been teaching ever since I was released from prison. They gathered together, ready to celebrate and praise the Lord in unity, but I had a different message for them than I usually did. Thinking of the one man who had been so effective earlier that week, I told them that they needed to take the words that they heard and go out and share them with as many people as they could.

"You are called to higher standards, brothers and sisters," I argued. "It is impossible for you to merely come here and listen but not act. I know that many of you don't have much confidence, but God has called you, and He will lead you. If you are working in your fields during the day, then practice by preaching to your cows. Work out God's message to the best of your ability. If you are in the forests, preach to the trees. If you are on a hill, preach to the grass."

I could see their faces sparking with new ideas and excitement. After they left that night, the message went forth like lightning in every direction—further and faster than it had ever gone before. Almost without exception, those who were in that group of five hundred went on to become missionaries, evangelists, and pastors in some of the most remote areas of China.

19

Fangcheng House Church

I was not always free to minister full-time. Because of my political status, I was still being pulled for work details. I often spent time working on road construction projects where I was digging in the hot summer sun. But when I was not working on road construction or preaching in secret underground meetings, I was taking every advantage to study God's Word and the history of Christianity in China.

Fangcheng County was rich with the history of Christians from other nations who had come to proclaim the gospel to the Chinese, and the area had been watered by the blood of martyrs. In 1807, a British missionary by the name of Robert Morrison arrived in Macau. It was not until almost eighty years later that another missionary arrived in Fangcheng, but even after much effort on his part, only one person had come to believe in Jesus Christ.

In 1909, the first church was built in Fangcheng; the following year, a second one was built that had a congregation of almost sixty believers. In 1914, a third church was built in Zhaofugang with ninety-three believers; and in 1919, a fourth church was constructed in Guaihe with a hundred and sixty-nine believers. Later, from 1950 to 1980, there was a thirty-year period of dormancy for our church in Fangcheng County. But the seeds that had been latent underground during that winter were now springing up with zest.

By 1981, the church body in Fangcheng was reminiscent of these words from Ezekiel:

> *The hand of the LORD was upon me, and he brought me out in the Spirit of the LORD and set me down in the middle of the valley; it was full of bones. And he led me around among them, and behold, there were very many on the surface of the valley, and behold, they were very dry. And he said to me, "Son of man, can these bones live?" And I answered, "O Lord GOD, you know." Then he said to me, "Prophesy over these bones, and say to them, O dry bones, hear the word of the LORD. Thus says the Lord GOD to these bones: Behold, I will cause breath to enter you, and you shall live. And I will lay sinews upon you, and will cause flesh to come upon you, and cover you with skin, and put breath in you, and you shall live, and you shall know that I am the LORD."*
>
> (Ezekiel 37:1–6)

Every town and village where I traveled to preach the gospel was seeing unimaginable growth in numbers of believers. Local leaders were rising up to take responsibility for their own areas and would preach and teach until I was able to return. I soon found myself branching out to locations that were further and further away, so that the geographical area in which I ministered was expanding significantly. This meant that I was not able to visit some areas as often as I liked, because my time was being divided more and more. This put a lot more responsibility on the local fellowships.

Every town and village where I traveled to preach the gospel was seeing unimaginable growth in numbers of believers.

We were a loose fellowship of believers, but I wanted everyone to feel unified in Christ, so I called a leadership meeting on October 1, 1981. October 1 is the start of a weeklong holiday in China celebrating the Communist Party. We chose this day to meet because most people would be free to attend. Every corner of Fangcheng now had a branch of leadership focusing on ministry in its local areas. It was amazing what God had done in only a short time and under some of the harshest conditions. At this meeting, there were over four hundred representatives in attendance who had seemingly sprouted up out of nowhere.

A repressive regime hell-bent on destroying the body of Christ in China had not only failed, but failed spectacularly! The church had not been destroyed. It had not even been downsized. It was increasing with a fury that had never been seen before in the history of Fangcheng.

Each of the four hundred leaders who came to the meeting represented individual church bodies throughout Fangcheng. When the meeting started, we all cried out to God in unison. Our prayer seemed to stretch out longer than usual. At about ten o'clock, the back door of the room burst open. Several dozen police officers swarmed in, armed with guns pointed right at us. "Police! Police!" I heard the commanding voice of the uniformed officers shouting. We had been caught. We had taken every precaution to ensure that the meeting would be safe, but it was just too difficult to arrange a meeting with four hundred people in a small village without someone finding out about it.

Suddenly, in a seemingly crazy act, I yelled out to everyone, "Do not fear. Do not fear. They cannot hurt you. They are mere men, and what can man do to you? Stand still and see how our heavenly Father will protect you. The One who is on our side is much bigger than they." I continued to preach. The crowd stopped paying attention to the police and instead listened to what I was saying.

The police yelled, "Shut up!" but I kept preaching, and the believers just smiled and continued to listen. "Do you understand that we are here to arrest you and put you in prison for religious superstition and participating in unsanctioned meetings?" The commanding officer looked around, perplexed by the lack of authority he seemed to have. Then he looked at his men, who were losing confidence in their command and authority. He reached to his side, pulled out his sidearm, and held it up. It was a last-ditch effort to show that he was indeed the one in charge. "One last time, I am commanding you to shut up!"

I continued to preach. The commanding officer didn't know how to react. I didn't know how to react either; I just trusted in the Lord. The officer then called the Religious Affairs Bureau, the government office in charge of religious activities, and a high-ranking official arrived at the meeting. He asked me, "May I speak with you?"

"Yes," I replied. I did not want to be belligerent. I just didn't want to shun my belief in Jesus in the face of punishment. Every part of my body wanted to obey the command of the officer, who was only upholding the laws of China, but the laws of China unfortunately ran in direct conflict with my belief in Jesus Christ.

Jesus gave very few commands, but He was very clear about this command: "*Go therefore and make disciples of all nations, baptizing them in the name of the Father and of the Son and of the Holy Spirit, teaching them to observe all that I have commanded you. And behold, I am with you always, to the end of the age*" (Matthew 28:19–20).

"I must be honest with you," the Bureau officer began. "The police have come here to catch you in the act of hosting an illegal religious meeting. I have come here to help you. Will you allow me to help you?"

"All we have in here are God's people. We are not criminals. We are honest citizens who desire to worship God together." After looking at him, I made a request. "Can we pray together before we start?"

"Uh, of course," he said.

I prayed over all of us. I asked for God's wisdom. I asked for His protection. I prayed in confidence, but I didn't know what the result of that night would be. I had no guaranties of anything. I knew only that God would reside in His people.

As soon as I ended the prayer, the Bureau official spoke out. "You are not supposed to be doing this. You can't just proclaim your God's name in a place where people do not believe." Just then, one of the sisters, Xiuling Ding, also known as Ding Hei, replied, "Sir, today we didn't proclaim the name of our Lord in the presence of those who do not believe—you did! Everyone here believes in the one and true God, but you have come in and tried to enforce your theory of no God."

"You cannot stay here. Everyone must leave. You cannot continue this meeting. This is pretty simple to understand."

"No, it is not so simple," I replied. "We have rights. We have the right to sing praises to our God. We have the liberty to enjoy fellowship with others who are also believers. We will not leave here until we are finished."

I knew the real reason why the police had come. They had come to arrest our leaders, but obviously the crowd was bigger than they had originally anticipated. We continued our meeting while the police waited for us outside. They were able to arrest only three representatives of the newly established Fangcheng leadership that night, but we were able to do what we had originally set out to accomplish: We had solidified a core leadership for the Fangcheng House Church that was unified in purpose and vision.

20

Revival Fires

Although things were booming for the church, the war on Christians in China had not ceased. It was actually relaunching. Previously, China had conducted a campaign that openly sought the destruction of all Christians, churches, and Christian materials. But the government had corrected its missteps and mistakes of the past. This time, it was launching a new blitz of raids and terror, but it was coupled with a media campaign, as well as foreign engagement for the purpose of cutting off the supply route from any allies.

In 1981, Chairman Deng Xiaoping opened new doors for China. He created a policy that allowed some people to claim property in order to build new homes, so that every family would have its own nest and could work to have a worry-free life. This was also a crucial moment in Chinese church history, because Christian workers who decided to give their lives to God and serve the church full-time had to make major decisions. Believers had to set their minds on long-term service, because unlike the "worry-free life" that was being promoted by the New China, the life of a church worker was going to be much different. We didn't make the same promises. Christians could anticipate suffering rather than ease.

The truth was, once Christians were identified as pastors or evangelists, they would not be able to return to their homes in the same way again. Time with their families would be numbered in hours per year. Safety would be only a relative term. Several young people stepped forward to accept their fate in the hands of the Lord. They were determined to preach the gospel and to lead the new flock in China, no matter what the future held. I had made the same decision years earlier, but there had been fewer of us then. Now, the number of people who were committing themselves was growing exponentially.

> ## China is a big country with a massive population, and we would see a change only if we sent out teams to every corner of the nation.

A team of people was coming together. I was inspired by the Scriptures that taught about Abraham putting together a team to go and rescue Lot from the hands of the enemy. (See Genesis 14:8–16.) I was also inspired by the seventy disciples whom Jesus sent out. (See Luke 10:1–12, 17–20.) God's Spirit spoke to me and told me that China is a big country with a massive population, and we would see a change only if we sent out teams to every corner of the nation.

From that point on, I was focused on evangelism and missions. In the beginning, we were only surviving. The gospel message had spread throughout all of Fangcheng County, yet we had not really had a focused strategy that we had planned out or written down. It had just happened. But now God was raising up a team from Fangcheng County to be sent out to reach the rest of China. Our steps were more purposeful than ever; long-term strategies, though in their infancy stage, were forming and feeding our ambitious desire to see God's kingdom expand. The momentum was strong and was roaring throughout the rural areas of China. The revival winds seemed completely unstoppable.

The team of evangelists did not have much money for travel. They were sent out with one-way train tickets and had little or no support waiting for them at their destinations. They were essentially journeying into the unknown. Traveling was not as easy then as it is now. We didn't have mobile phones, e-mail, or other electronic communication to coordinate departures and arrivals. We were not able to mail letters to one another because not only was the practice itself unsafe, but making long-term plans by post did not allow the flexibility we needed to remain safe. Setting up times and places for meetings was also not easily coordinated, especially when we were going to places and locations that didn't have electricity.

Once the team members arrived at their destinations, they immediately began to preach the gospel and to plant churches. They were able to set up churches in the provinces of Henan, Hubei, and Anhui. Baptism centers were established in the most central locations so that new believers could be baptized quickly. Soon, new Christians were being baptized every day in record numbers. Within only a short period of time, as many as two thousand believers per day were being baptized.

In addition, during the 1980s, foreigners began coming into China again. The restrictions implemented by Mao Zedong were slowly being relaxed; as a result, there were increasing numbers of visitors—tour groups, investors, and missionaries who were pretending to be tourists and teachers. Suddenly, missionaries were coming into China from Hong Kong, Taiwan, Europe, and America. These zealous believers had a burden for China; the nation had been closed to the world for decades, and they wanted to find out what the current situation of the church was.

We desperately needed their help. We had so little teaching from the Bible, and very few of us even had access to Bibles. For example, when we were teaching about the book of Acts, the word for "Acts" sounded to us like the Chinese word for "stone," so we taught that God would make disciples out of stones. We read the Bible on our own and tried to understand as much of it as we could. The Holy Spirit helped us and kept us from the many dangers that we could have encountered in such a situation. There were so many times when the enemy could have led us astray, but the Lord protected us from falling into heresy.

We didn't have teaching materials, history books, or the like. We only had preaching from the few of us who had our own Bibles. I would preach a message, and the leaders would listen to it and write down as much as they were able to, and then they would run to the next village and deliver the message. So many doors were left wide open for apostasy. It really is a miracle how the church grew. The church was moving faster, further, and deeper than ever, and I was busy preaching more than I ever had before.

Because we didn't have many Bibles or teachers, it was necessary for me to travel every day to preach. Churches were growing daily, and fellowships were popping up in every town and village. I went to as many as five fellowships per day, and never less than two. The people were so hungry that they would gather and wait until I arrived, no matter how long they had to wait. And not only was I preaching at the meetings, but I was also performing weddings, funerals, and baptisms every day. I had no background in performing ceremonies, and at first it felt odd and awkward, but after a while it felt completely natural.

Everywhere I went, I would be surrounded by hungry, passionate believers who were willing to do anything, to go anywhere, and to risk any danger in order to hear the Word preached.

The first few months of these activities were absolutely exhilarating. God had answered all my prayers. I had prayed that He would open the hearts of my countrymen. I had prayed and prayed for revival fires to fall upon all of China. Now I could see that God was answering those petitions. Revival was falling like rain, and I was on a perpetual high. I would run from village to village with excitement and urgency. Before I would finish one service, I would already be geared up for the next one. It was hard for me to sleep or to eat. Everywhere I went, I would be surrounded by hungry, passionate believers who were willing to do anything, to go anywhere, and to risk any danger in order to hear the Word preached.

Even when I was tired and could feel myself coming down from an emotional and spiritual high, I would be reenergized by the adrenaline flowing from the crowd. It was like drinking bottled energy. But as time went on, my energy boosts became shorter and shorter, and my downtimes became longer and longer. Energy seemed to seep out of me onto the floor, and there was no way I could scoop it up and put it back inside me. I was utterly exhausted and in desperate need of rejuvenation; my body needed rest, my mind needed respite, and my spirit needed serenity. "God," I cried out, "please give me rest. I don't know how, but I need it." I didn't have much of a background in theology, so I didn't have a mind-set that restricted what I thought God could or could not do. I did not know how He would eventually answer my prayer.

Three days after I had prayed to God that I was in desperate need of rest, I finally found the break that I was looking for—in a form that I never would have imagined. I came down with a high fever, and all ministering had to stop at once. The fever grew higher and higher. It confined me to my bed. People prayed for me but nothing changed. After months of praying without seeing any results, many people quietly began to think that I was going to die. They expected it to happen before long.

Things were so dire that at one point, a member of our church was passing by a funeral service and looked up to see a woman, also from our church, weeping at the funeral. He automatically assumed that I had died but that he hadn't heard about it, so he took a seat at the back of the funeral service and began to cry, too, asking the Lord why He had taken me away so soon!

The fever confined me to my bed for six months. Even though I was technically sick, it was as if my body knew that it needed rest and had thus shut down everything else, keeping my movements restricted. After this, my fever rose to new levels and became really dangerous. People gathered around me and prayed for several hours. I repented of all my sins and was prepared to die, but within a short time, my temperature came down and I was completely well. Since that day, I have never once complained about being too busy.

21

Intense Persecution

On August 16, 1983, the government started a new push to eliminate underground house churches. China was adjusting to its new leadership, things had settled down, and the authorities were back on the rampage against Christians. Their first target, of course, was the underground house church network in Fangcheng. This network was growing every day, even though it was against the law for people to evangelize. Government leaders reasoned that churches should have died out long before 1980, so Fangcheng Church defied their logic. They concluded that it must be a conspiracy.

The persecution was swift and intense. The police began planning raids and executing them flawlessly. People were arrested every day, and churches were scattered. Many of the leaders from Fangcheng Church were arrested and beaten. The police were looking for the main leader—me. They were arresting members of the church and torturing them in an attempt to find out all the details of how we operated, where we operated, and how we were financing it all. Fangcheng Church had become public enemy number one. This, of course, elevated me to the top of the hit list.

With the sudden onslaught of arrests and beatings, we did what we do best in bad times—we prayed. The church called out to God for supernatural protection and mercy. We all fell on our knees and cried out to Him for His sovereign leadership and guidance through the tempest.

More and more of my companions were arrested. Raids were occurring with amazing accuracy. The police seemed to know our steps before we took them. We tried to change tactics and be more secretive about our meetings, but they still found us. Within only a few months, the police had rounded up most of the major leadership. But by the winter of 1983, the police were no longer interested in arresting anyone. They had learned more about the leadership than they had wanted to know and were astounded at the growth of the church. The interrogations of the Christians whom they had arrested had given them information that they had never dreamed of. The situation was much worse than anyone in the government had imagined. The authorities circulated information on the main leaders of Fangcheng Church and issued orders for them to be shot on sight.

> **Raids were occurring with amazing accuracy. The police seemed to know our steps before we took them.**

From the interrogations, they had identified thirteen leaders whom they felt needed to be immediately removed from society by any means possible. The police sent out a list of all thirteen leaders. Signs that read "Wanted, dead or alive" with the thirteen names were posted throughout Fangcheng. The police found them all and shot them. Yet these leaders had already committed themselves to the Lord. They were already dead in Christ, and it was Christ who lived in them.

Young men and women who boldly followed Christ had to come to terms early on in their faith that they were most likely not going to live very long. This was just a fact of life in 1983. It was not a pessimistic outlook or a view that lacked faith in Christ. Accordingly, the believers felt it was their obligation to help their family members and friends find gravesites for their own burial and to prepare their funeral arrangements so that they would not be a financial burden to their loved ones.

Though they prepared for their own deaths, they were not filled with gloom. They willingly made the choice to follow Christ because He gave them hope and joy, salvation and true life. To be ready for death was to be free from fear. Fear couldn't hold these believers down. They knew that the grave was not the end but the beginning.

It was clear that Christians were fair game in China, and anyone who wanted to slaughter them was encouraged to do just that. Many Christians were being shot and left for dead, but I was the one they wanted the most. The police saturated the villages with signs and informants in order to gain information about me, but they were not able to get close enough to catch me.

One night, we were all gathered in a secret meeting and there was a heaviness on our hearts because of what the believers were suffering. The persecution was intense, and tomorrow hadn't been promised to anyone. As we were praying, a young man by the name of Shuqian Zheng suddenly bolted to his feet and said, "What are you scared of? What is there to fear? God is in control, and He will take care of us. We are His. Brothers and sisters, we are His co-laborers; we are His friends. I can see the Spirit of the Lord moving through China like a mighty wind that no one can stop. There will be a day when Chinese Christians will prosper in ways that cannot be imagined today. There will be a day when the Chinese people will have a car for every home and a home for every family."

Brother Shuqian got even more excited and animated as he spoke. The Spirit of the Lord was moving through him. "One day, the Lord's glory will shine on the Chinese people. One day, horror, poverty, and tears will be replaced with peace, wealth, and laughter." His words seemed absolutely impossible to grasp at that time, but they were prophetic regarding what God was going to do in China. As soon as Brother Shuqian was finished speaking, everyone began to sing,

> I am unsure of what tomorrow will bring, but I will live for the
>   Lord each day.
> I don't have to worry about tomorrow, because I trust in His
>   promise.
> One thing that I know above all else is that I am going to be
>   walking together with the Lord.
> There are so many things that I cannot comprehend now,
> but I know who is in control and who always holds my hand.

After this, Ding Hei, the woman who had replied to the Bureau official when the police raided our leadership meeting, helped us to ride out the night by keeping us calm. "Trust in the Lord," she cried out until we were all calm and at peace. Ding Hei, who was nicknamed "Sister D," was born in Fangcheng County in 1961. Her father was a local cadre with the Communist Party, and her mother was a Christian who had become a believer after secretly visiting a house church when Sister D was still a child.

Sister D became a believer when she was in middle school. She secretly shared the gospel with her classmates, and roughly forty of them got saved and met together after school to pray. If their teachers had known that they were secretly praying together, the students—as well as their family members—would have been in danger, so they would give each other discreet, secret signs during school about the meetings. Sister D would also spend hours by herself during which she would practice preaching the gospel. She worked on her technique and delivery so that when the opportunity presented itself, she would be able to share the gospel effectively. Interestingly, one day during school, Sister D and her fellow classmates were required to sit and watch my trial on TV. This was the first time she had seen a pastor accused in an open trial.

Sister D's father was very abusive and forbade her to participate in any Christian meetings. When she was a little older, she ran away from home and never returned. She traveled over the mountains to Guihe, where she was able to meet with me. Sister D lived with our family for more than six years. She was one of our very first full-time workers in Fangcheng, and she developed a reputation for openly defying the authorities. She was an incredible preacher and had no fear of being detained.

"A bullet costs 0.15 renminbi," she once said at a small gathering of believers. "If we are executed, the government will make our family pay for the bullet used to execute us. Let's make it worth the price that our families will have to pay. We owe so much to our Lord. As long as we are alive, let us not waste one minute. We have only a limited time to share the gospel before we are caught and executed, so let's not burn daylight wasting time. There are so many lost souls who need to be saved from the path leading to hell. This is the best way to spend our time, and, dare I say it, the best way to give our lives."

Her words struck a chord with everyone there. The room was electrified. All the believers were ready to lay down their lives for the sake of the gospel, even if the cost at the end of the day was 0.15 renminbi. In that moment, they came together in a special show of unity and pledged their lives to serve the Lord, forming what became known as the "Dare to Die Team." This team was made up of a group of

"We have only a limited time to share the gospel before we are caught and executed, so let's not burn daylight wasting time."

fearless and courageous Christians who were ready to challenge the system in China in order to preach the gospel of Jesus Christ. They considered their lives to be worthless in and of themselves. Instead, their lives had value only in the eyes of their Creator, and so they lived in service to Him, even if it meant certain death.

After the thirteen leaders were hunted down and killed by the police, the burden to do even more for the gospel solidified in the hearts of the Dare to Die Team. About thirty people in all joined. These were all impressive young men and women who were only about twenty to thirty years old. The oldest was just over forty-five. They dispersed to different locations in China without any fear of death.

Sister D was part of the Dare to Die Team and didn't reserve any kind words for the Party officials or their activities. She not only played an important role in the church in general, but she also played a key role for Christian women in China.

During the Cultural Revolution, women were elevated from their submissive roles in China and given equal roles with men in the labor force. Previously, Chinese women had been kept in subservient roles that were reinforced by certain practices, such as the binding of feet. Now China was full of banners and posters picturing women working in the factories and fields.

As the church in China began to explode, the number of women outnumbered the number of men. Many people in the church did not know how the women should behave, but Sister D was able to lead by example. She displayed an amazing tact and humility in dealing with others, and at the same time, she strongly showed the way for women. Many of the women were able to observe the trail she blazed and find their own places in the church.

Generations of women learned from Sister D's example and found comfort in her leadership. Most of the time in China, women were getting saved even though their husbands were against it. Sister D was able to raise up an army of women who were responsible for bringing their husbands and their entire families to the Lord.

Sister D led the Dare to Die Team to far-flung areas in rural China. Two by two, preachers were sent out to places in the provinces of Henan, Sichuan, Hubei, Hunan, Shanxi, Anhui, Jiangsu, and Shandong. We had little money to give them, so they were sent out with only about twenty-five U.S. cents per person for noodles. They were going to have to rely on God for their needs. They were going to have to live by faith and trust in the Lord in order to survive day by day.

These teams laid the foundation for one of the largest revivals the world has ever seen. The power of the Holy Spirit resided upon them. The Holy Spirit called them and sustained them. The teams went out over a period of six months to two years, preaching the gospel in areas that did not speak Mandarin Chinese, did not share the culture of the Han Chinese (the largest ethnic group in China) and held deeply seated animosity against the Han.

When they returned to Fangcheng, we did not recognize them. Their hair was matted from weeks of not being washed. They were malnourished and much thinner. Their skin was leathery, having been darkened by the sun and chapped by the harsh winds of western China. Their sacrifice was tangible, but so were the fruits of their labors. Before the ambassadors from the Dare to Die Team went out, the impact of the revival in Fangcheng was mainly contained within the borders of that county; but after the team left, revival fires were lit all over the place and burned independently.

One example of the Dare to Die Team's effect is what occurred in a town called Nankai in Sichuan. The minority group in Nankai worshipped a tree. They believed that the tree was a god and that if the people touched it, they would die. When team members entered the town, they were immediately introduced to the tree. Proving that they had duly earned the title "Dare to Die," they touched the tree. They showed no fear of the tree god because they knew that the God whom they served was much greater than anything in the world.

The team members boldly announced that Jesus was Lord of all and that they would release the people from any future burden related to the tree—then they cut down the tree. The locals were shocked, but at the same time, they felt free from fear. So many of the locals had been afraid that their children would accidentally touch the tree and be punished in their ignorance.

The Dare to Die team laid the foundation for one of the largest revivals the world has ever seen.

After the Dare to Die members cut down the tree, the village waited to see what would happen to them. Many villagers were certain that the Christians would be struck dead at any moment, but the evangelists stood where the tree once stood and declared the power of the Lord over all things. The villagers listened to every word. This was no small thing for them. Almost every villager came forward to become a follower of Jesus Christ.

This demonstration of God's power took place everywhere the Dare to Die Team went. Chinese idols that the locals had thought were all-powerful proved to be no match for the true and living God. People saw that the God of the Dare to Die Team was real and alive. The sick were healed, the crippled were restored, and the blind regained their sight.

It was not long before the authorities began hearing about the Dare to Die Team's activities. Posters of known Christian evangelists participating in the team were displayed everywhere. They could be seen on every corner in Nanyang and throughout the county of Fangcheng. A reward of fifteen hundred U.S. dollars was offered to anyone who could report on any activities that would lead to the arrest of one of these evangelists. The hunt was on.

22

Underground Networks

As the growth of new believers spread to additional areas, we learned that other church networks were forming in Anhui Province, located east of Henan Province and west of Shanghai. We had been helping the churches in Anhui for several years by sharing Bibles with them, but I had never had the chance to travel there and meet with any believers.

We had started delivering Bibles to Anhui in 1983. Five years later, I was invited to visit the province, meet with the church leadership, and preach the gospel in the churches there. The church that invited me was in Yingshang County, Anhui. Like Fangcheng, the Yingshang Church Network had expanded into other areas of China, and those new churches were called by the name of that county, too. In fact, Yingshang County was exploding with new believers and was sparking revival elsewhere. When I arrived there, I realized why. The leaders, Xiaofu Chen and Zhanghe Chen, were humble men who were hungry for God's Word.

These leaders gave me such a warm welcome, and it was so nice to be with them. I really felt like I was with members of my own family in Fangcheng. Not long after I arrived, the leadership led me to a body of believers that had gathered in a small area; I was expected to speak right away. When I started to introduce myself, I noticed that each and every face was glued to me. All the believers were sitting on the edge of their seats and listening carefully to every word I said. The air was electric with expectation. I could see the eagerness in their faces, as if they wanted to reach up and pull the words out of my mouth in case they did not come out fast enough.

I shouted out into the rain, praying blessings upon each one. We were not hiding now but out in the open. None of us were afraid.

I was not able to speak for very long. Simultaneously, almost as if on cue, all the believers raised their hands in praise. Soon, we all began to vocalize our praise. Then we moved into deeper worship; in that moment, the presence of God filled the room, and all of us fell on our faces. We cried out together in unison. We begged for forgiveness and then tangibly felt the waters of forgiveness wash us clean. The power of the Lord was absolute, and we were not able to think about anything else for the next two days.

On the second afternoon, I realized that it was already time for me to return to Henan Province. All the believers were on their faces, praying, so I slowly stood to my feet. I really wanted to hug them before I left and tell them how meaningful my time with them had been, but so many of them had tears streaming down their faces, and I could not bring myself to interrupt their personal time with Jesus.

I turned and silently walked out the door. I saw that it was raining, so I pulled my jacket tight around my body, put my head down, held up my umbrella, and stepped out into the rain. I did not make it far before I heard the door open behind me. "Zhang!" a voice yelled. I turned to see someone come running out the door, yelling my name and raising his hand to get my attention. My heart was moved to see that he was not concerned about the rain at all.

Then, like a swarm of bees, many more believers came rushing out the door. It looked like more than a hundred people were trying to fit through the doorway at the same time. They all came running out into the rain, calling my name. One by one, they ran up to me as close as they could and then fell to their knees in the mud, saying, "Lay hands on us, please, Pastor Zhang! Please don't leave us without blessing us."

As if by reflex, I threw my umbrella into the mud and began to lay hands on them. I shouted out into the rain, praying blessings upon each one. We were not hiding now but out in the open. None of us were afraid. We were concentrating only on the power of the Lord and on the goodness that He gives. In all the years that I have been preaching the gospel in China, none of the prayer times have been more precious than that one.

Before I left, I said my final words to the leader, Pastor Chen. His body was erect as I said farewell. He had a boldness to proclaim the gospel bravely. In fact, I could see that Pastor Chen had unusual boldness in declaring the Word of God. I knew that I would be working together with Yingshang Church for many years to come. The Yingshang County underground house church network eventually became known as the "Truth Network." We were able to unite to establish churches throughout China and to spread the Word of God into the most remote areas.

The church in Yingshang County was very similar to the church in Tanghe County, which is about seventy miles from Fangcheng. Pastor Jianguo Feng, the founder of the underground house church network in Tanghe, had many things in common with Pastor Chen in Anhui. Both were men of passion and zeal for preaching the cross.

I didn't know Pastor Chen as well as I knew Pastor Feng. I had spent three and a half years with Pastor Feng in prison. Spending time in prison with someone really helps you to get to know who they are. I had seen him in his most vulnerable state, as he had seen me in mine. During those years, we had laughed together, cried together, and suffered together. I had drawn much of my strength from him, as he had from me. We had encouraged each other when times were unbearable and we wanted to die. God had placed Pastor Feng in the same prison cell as me to save my life. During the hardest and darkest moments, Pastor Feng had shared God's Word with me, and it had given me new life. I had so many fond memories of sleeping under the stars in the fields with Pastor Feng as we waited to sneak out of the prison to go and preach in the small rural villages, and I could see the same characteristics in Pastor Chen.

God was preparing the three of us to lead one of the largest revivals that China had ever seen. And we were not the only ones He was preparing. Another pastor in Anhui Province who was associated with Pastor Chen had gained a reputation for preaching. Additionally, a pastor by the name of Xianqi Zheng had been traveling around and planting churches in Lixin County, Anhui. The churches in Lixin County, like those of Tanghe County, Fangcheng County, and Yingshang County, were blazing through the countryside with the fires of revival.

No one could ever have imagined that we "criminals" would be used by God to change the social and spiritual landscape of the Chinese nation.

Lixin County Church later became known as "Blessing" underground house church network. Pastor Zheng was also full of boldness, courageously facing the consequences of preaching the gospel in China. I was able to meet with him for the first time when Pastor Dennis Balcombe from America introduced us. I quickly learned that Pastor Zheng had the same faith and the same vision that I had, and that he'd gone through similar experiences. Even though we had never worked together or even met before, we were able to find immediate common ground in the Word of God.

Again, God was moving among these very simple men to initiate one of the largest revivals that China—and the world—had ever seen. No one could ever have imagined that we "criminals" would be used by God to change the social and spiritual landscape of the Chinese nation. Pastors Feng, Chen, and I would collaborate to bring all of China the gospel of Jesus Christ, and Pastor Zheng would subsequently join us. The Fangcheng, Yingshang, and Tanghe County churches would later be estimated to have a combined membership of about thirty million believers spread all over China.

The house churches were being formed into a fierce body of believers. I want to mention one more network from Henan Province that was moving like a firestorm. In Nanyang County, there was a radical underground house church that soon became known as the "Born Again Movement." This was one of the first networks not to be named after its county of origin. The leader of the church was Xu Yongzi, also known as Peter Xu.

The first time I met Peter Xu was in 1980, at a meeting where many companions had come together. At that time, the people were not very passionate, and most of the Christians came from Nanyang. The Nanyang believers were a blessing to the church in Henan. When I first laid eyes on Peter, I could tell that he was fiery and passionate. His ability to communicate the gospel was unique. Not many preachers or pastors could to communicate the message with as much clarity and conviction as Peter was able to. His words flowed so smoothly.

As I watched him and listened to his messages, I noted that he was more academic than anyone I had ever heard before; additionally, in only a short time, he was able to plan, organize, and mobilize large numbers of believers. Peter was an amazing organizer, and all of us admired him. I felt that Peter Xu was a great blessing to the Chinese church. He was quite devoted, and his family had suffered for the sake of Christ; they really felt the burden of Peter's service to the church. His sister and his sons have also been set apart to serve the Lord.

Many groups came out of the Born Again Movement. Peter's church was made up of so many passionate evangelists, many of whom were in the city of Nanyang. And the church had already started to send out evangelists to regions throughout China.

We didn't know much at that time, but one of the few things we were certain of was that God was moving in China and that, for some reason unclear to any of us, He was using us in an unusual way. These simple underground house church networks were coming together to form a special relationship that would change the entire social balance of China.

23

Unifying the Churches

When the Spirit of the Lord moved upon the churches in China, thousands began to flood into the kingdom. I was running to keep up with the growth, but I recognized that something was missing. I felt a strong burden for unity. The church in China didn't have the luxury of being divided; we needed to be united against the enemy that was attacking us on a regular basis. The Chinese government was spreading false information about us to believers around the world, and it was attempting to isolate the church networks one by one so that we could be conquered. The only way we could survive this attack was to come together and stand united in the Lord's strength.

In 1994, God stirred my heart to help bring unity to the churches. I began to pray about it and to discuss it with others. It seemed impossible at that time. How could we bring the leaders of the underground organizations together? The police had been scouring the countryside for years looking for the leadership of these networks, which the government publicly claimed didn't even exist. Putting us all together in the same room at the same time would be a rare prize for the authorities if they discovered us.

Nevertheless, God had put this burning desire for unity in my heart, and against all odds, I was ready to see how He would move. The Lord had given me the name of "Sinim" for our joint fellowship. The word comes from Isaiah 49, and many people believe that it refers to China. *"Behold,*

*these shall come from afar—and, behold, these from the north and from the
west, and these from the land of Sinim"* (Isaiah 49:12 AMP).

In 1996, things started to fall into place. I contacted a couple of our
brothers, and we began to pray for unity among all the underground
house churches in China. On November 8, 1996, I was able to meet with
the leaders of the other major networks at a gathering in Pingdingshan
Township, Henan Province. We
were coming together for the very
first time to dedicate ourselves to
unity. Yinxiang and Lixin from
Anhui Province were not in attendance at that meeting because they
had not yet made a decision to join
with us. Yinxiang, also called the
Truth Network, was experiencing
changes in its fellowship. Because
of both persecution and rapid
growth, it had a constant turnover
of leadership. It was not until Chen
became established as the leader that they were able to make a strong decision about joining our united fellowship.

**God had put this burning desire
for unity in my heart, and
against all odds, I was ready to
see how He would move.**

There was another challenge. Some of the groups did not want to be
closely associated with Peter Xu or Pastor Enoch Wang, a well-known
network leader in Henan Province. While they acknowledged these men's
work, they were concerned about some of their theology. Peter Xu's group
was being labeled the "weepers." This term seemed to stem from a require-
ment to cry during prayer. The other leaders did not agree with the network's emphasis that linked physical tears with true spiritual repentance.
Peter Xu was concerned about our groups, as well. He was more conser-
vative than the rest of us in the house church movement with regard to
spiritual gifts.

In addition, some of the leaders had reservations about Enoch Wang
because he didn't use the same Bible as everyone else. The majority of the
churches in China use the *Chinese Union Version* Bible and consider it to be
a trustworthy translation. However, Enoch Wang and his group translated

their own version. This led to them to adopt some ideas about the Holy Trinity that were controversial and caused further disagreements.

I truly believed that we needed to include Peter Xu and Enoch Wang in order to begin the process of unity. What power is there in unity if we are all exactly the same? Unity has a special potency when people are able to come together in spite of their differences. We were different in our approach to worship and preaching, but we were united in our belief in Jesus Christ. We were also united in our unfortunate common circumstances of being persecuted and hunted by the government.

I felt that the only way I could bring in Peter Xu was to ask him to be the chairman of the fellowship. I don't think he would have joined if I had been chairman. I also thought that if Peter were given that position, we would most likely secure the participation of Pastor Wang. Prior to the meeting, I had communicated my idea to appoint Peter Xu as chairman, and during the meeting we were able to make it official.

At first, due to the abovementioned concerns, the other leaders had challenged me about bringing in Peter Xu and Enoch Wang. But I shared with them that it would be to everyone's benefit if they were included. "Wouldn't it be better if we were able to bring them into a relationship with us so that they can know their shortcomings?" I argued. "If you disagree with them and abandon them, will they not continue going down that road? But what if we bring them into our fellowship and listen to them, and they listen to us? Maybe then we will have a chance to change them a little bit at a time."

Brother Yun, who is now well-known worldwide as "the Heavenly Man," which is also the title of his biography, was enthusiastic about all of us uniting to share the Word of God, so we put him in charge of missions for our fellowship. We might not have realized it at the time, but we were making Chinese history together. Never before had so many Christians existed in China, and never before had so many Chinese believers been unified in heart, vision, and purpose.

We began praying together right away, and as we prayed, God once more brought to mind Isaiah 49:12. As I wrote previously, many people believe that the word "*Sinim*" in this verse signifies China. China is often referred to as *Sinim* or *Sino* with regard to diplomatic relationships, such as in the term "Sino-American relations." Thus, we agreed to call ourselves the Sinim Fellowship; it became our "official" effort to promote unity among the underground house churches in China. The name was important because if we had included the word *China* in the title, there would likely have been political repercussions. People might well have interpreted our fellowship as a secret political group that had been formed to overthrow the government, much as Mao Zedong had done. We did not want to overthrow the government. We simply wanted to follow Christ freely. The Sinim Fellowship gave us a specific identity that people could associate with the underground churches as we channeled our message to the outside world. It also gave us a way to speak officially when we were attacked. That small meeting in Pingdingshan Village was a pivotal, landmark meeting.

> We did not want to overthrow the government. We simply wanted to follow Christ freely.

All of us were excited about working together and about the promise of unity. On January 16, 1997, shortly before the Chinese New Year festivities, we were able to meet together again. This time, more than three hundred believers were in attendance representing the leadership of the Sinim Fellowship networks. One of the main speakers at the meeting was Enoch Wang. Enoch's Spirit-filled preaching filled our hearts with excitement that day, but it was the songbird Xiao Min who truly solidified us all in spirit.

God has used Xiao Min to touch the underground house church in an amazing way. She grew up as a poor farm girl and never attended secondary school. She cannot read music, but somehow she has written more than one thousand songs that are known around the world as "the Canaan Hymns." Her songs are a pure expression of the gospel as understood by the Chinese underground church, and her words communicate our thoughts and feelings. Accordingly, at the Sinim Fellowship meeting, the entire body of believers was lost in the praise and worship she led us in.

I had met Xiao Min for the first time in 1989 at a meeting in Macheng Village, in northeastern Hubei Province, at which I was preaching. I noticed a young girl there who was very much an introvert yet absolutely lost in the moment as she praised God. She was surrounded by people on every side, yet she was somehow all alone with God. She had a unique quality that made her shine, so that she stood out from everyone else.

I heard that she had been writing songs, and I knew that this was something Fangcheng church desperately needed. Many of our songs were carryovers from the hymns and songs that had been brought over by the foreign missionaries to China. We were not very familiar with the tunes and did not know how they were supposed to sound or what words we should use with them. Xiao Min's songs gave life to our praise. She helped us to articulate our own experiences and desires before the Lord. Consequently, her music became a key element in the growth of all five of the house churches in the Sinim Fellowship. I would even go so far as to say that the Chinese church would not be what it is today if God had not moved in the heart of this shy, uneducated, young farm girl. He inspired her to tell the story of the underground house church with honesty and purity. She is a treasure for believers in China, but she is also a blessing to Chinese churches all around the world who sing her hymns.

During our Sinim gathering, Xiao Min moved the entire roomful of leaders when she began singing a song called "The Unity of the Church." The power of the lyrics stirred our spirits, and we all committed our lives to serve China and her church. She moved us again when she sang at another Sinim Fellowship meeting in June of the same year. At that meeting, Pastor Li Tianen taught about Chinese church history, and Xiao Min sang three songs: "We Become Winners," "Dove Flies Back," and "A Sky Without Fences."

When she sang "A Sky Without Fences," we were all humbled. The song speaks of the kingdom of God being a place without any barriers between churches, doctrines, cultures, languages, or creeds. Many of the barriers we contend with are man-made, self-inflicted obstacles that hinder the Word of God from going forth.

24

Confessing the Faith

The promise of unity was exciting, but the honeymoon was short-lived. Soon after word got around that the underground church was unifying, government persecution began again. In the 1990s, many foreigners believed that the existence of the underground house churches was a myth. This false belief was largely due to a Chinese government propaganda tactic that mouthpieces in the West were happy to repeat worldwide. A similar situation occurs today. When China wants to push a message, there is no shortage of mouthpieces in the West that will repeat the message to the rest of the world in hopes of finding favorable access to China's resources.

Before the Sinim Fellowship was formed, the networks other than Fangcheng were working independently throughout China and had little or no contact with Peter Xu or Enoch Wang. I was loosely associated with both sides, being connected with Peter and Enoch, as well as with the Tanghe network and the Anhui churches. I was able to see what challenges they were experiencing individually, but they were not really able to see each other.

The Sinim Fellowship gave us an opportunity to see how similar our churches really were. Even so, our differences echoed off the walls when we were together. It was hard to hide them, but we were all respectful of one another. For example, all of us charismatic preachers would be standing around ready to shout and praise the Lord with all our might, especially Brother Yun. He would practically bounce off the walls when he was preaching. He was always animated when he spoke, with his hands going up and down and back and forth. He would emphasize each Chinese word with gusto and charisma.

His style was in contrast to that of Peter Xu and Enoch Wang, who were both very somber and reflective when they spoke. They would often fold their hands in front of them and deliver their messages as if they were speaking to an official government body. When the other leaders prayed, they would pace back and forth and speak passionately. Peter and Enoch would remain stationary, their feet planted in one spot, when they petitioned the Lord on behalf of China.

Although our actions were different, we were united in our goals. Our meetings were secret, but they were open to all the underground house church fellowships. And although we were making history, our meetings were very relaxed.

We had decided to rotate the location of the Sinim Fellowship meetings. Each one would be hosted by a different network in sequence. On March 16, 1997, the Sinim Fellowship leaders received a note from Peter Xu about the next meeting. He requested that we all come together at a house he had rented. I knew that if he arranged the meeting, it would be safe, without concerns about security.

The meeting was being requested in part because a special guest, Sister Shu, was coming. Sister Shu was an older lady who had already retired. She was very well-known and was said to have carried favor with former Chairman Deng Xiaoping. Sister Shu had been living in America and was now returning to China for a visit.

I wanted to be at the meeting, but Pastor Shen Yiping and I had already arranged a secret meeting in Shanghai. All the other leaders traveled to meet with Sister Shu, but the meeting didn't turn out as planned. From what I was told, it seems that Sister Shu was not aware of the nature of security in China. After she arrived in the country, she was not completely sure how to get to the meeting place, so she stopped and asked the local police for directions! Once the police got wind of the meeting, they came in full force to arrest everyone there. In one fell swoop, they were able to capture some "big fish" that day, including Peter Xu, Enoch Wang, and

Brother Yun. We did not know it then, but the Sinim Fellowship would never be the same after that. The winds of persecution began to blow, and none of us were able to escape them. The unification of the underground church in China was the last thing that the enemy wanted to see, and when it became clear that we were all willing to set aside our differences for the purpose of the kingdom, the attacks came rolling in.

> The winds of persecution began to blow, and none of us were able to escape them.

I knew that it was only a matter of time before the police caught up with me, too, so we called together another Sinim Fellowship meeting. Our purpose was clear. We wanted to write a statement of faith that all of us could agree on and establish as an official statement of unity for the church in China. In November 1998, about twenty of us came together while Peter Xu was still in prison. We worked together to write a confession of faith, and a brother by the name of Cannon Zhao wrote it down. No foreigners were present during this meeting because we felt it was important that the statement of faith for the underground church remain as indigenous as possible.

We were all a sight to see during the two days it took us to write the confession. Each one of us was praying and studying his Bible, furiously looking for the perfect words to use to adequately represent our own beliefs, while at the same time not excluding any of the networks. I conclude this chapter with an abridged translation of that confession.

Unregistered Chinese House Church Confession of Faith

The Bible

We believe that all sixty-six scrolls throughout the Bible were revealed by God's Spirit, who had spoken to us through prophets and apostles.

The Bible contains the complete and perfect truth; it has the highest authority, and no one is allowed to add any words to it or take any away from it.

The Bible clearly proclaims God's wonderful plan for saving the human race, and it has set up the highest principles for our life and service. We resist any theory that would deny the Bible as God's words or suggest that the Bible is outdated or has mistakes and faults, or that only part of the Bible deserves to be trusted. We emphasize the relevance of reading the Bible in complete context and obeying the teaching and guidance of the Spirit of God to correctly teach others the message of God's truth.

The Bible supersedes our own opinions or thinking.

The Trinity

We believe in one true God. He is the God with the name "I Am who I Am"—Holy Father, Holy Son, Holy Spirit in One. In essence and in the nature, They are equally full of glory and honor. Though God is one, each Member of the Trinity has His own job: the Father plans for salvation, the Son accomplishes that salvation, the Spirit reveals that salvation. At the same time, we should know and remember that the Father, Son, and Spirit are inseparable. The Holy Son reveals to us the Father; by the Holy Spirit we know and see the Son. They are to be worshipped and praised. We pray to the Father through the Holy Spirit in the name of the Son.

We believe that God created the universe and everything in it. He made man in His likeness. With His great power, He sustains the universe and controls human history. Almighty God is a God of righteousness, holiness, faithfulness, and kindness. He knows all and dwells everywhere. The Holy Son and the Holy Spirit last forever. The Father begat the Son; the Father and the Son send the Holy Spirit to the world.

God is Spirit, and only by the power of His Spirit can people worship Him as He really is. He is the only God Christians are to worship.

Christ

We believe that Jesus Christ is God's only Son. He became flesh and came into the world. He was tempted as a human yet committed no sin. He was crucified willingly so that by His blood, we who believe in Him may be saved from the power of evil and from our sins. In three days, He was raised from the dead and is now sitting at the right hand of the Father our God. After having received the Spirit from the Father, He sent the Spirit to all who believe in Him. On the last day, Christ will come again and judge the world. Although Christians have become God's children through Jesus, yet they shall never be God. Nobody knows the exact date of Jesus' return, but we can be sure that Christ will come back. We are completely against the rumor saying that Christ has already come back in the flesh; if anyone claims that he is the second Christ, he is considered a cult.

Redemption

We believe that whoever admits and repents of his sin, acknowledges Jesus as God's only Son who died for man on the cross and was raised from death three days later so that our sins may be forgiven, and accepts the promised Spirit, will be born again and be saved. For it is by the grace of God that all are put right with God through faith. In faith, we are called the righteous people. In faith, we receive the Spirit. In faith, we are called the children of God.

We believe that God will keep us safe to the end in Jesus Christ; and conversely, believers must keep the message of God's truth to the end also.

We believe that the proof of our being saved is the Spirit's dwelling inside us. Meanwhile, God's Spirit, together with our hearts, proves that we are God's children.

The Holy Spirit

We believe that the Holy Spirit is the Spirit of God, of Christ, full of truth and holiness. The Holy Spirit enlightens the heart, revealing to us God's truth and convincing us that Christ Jesus is the Savior. He guides the saints on the path of Truth, helps saints understand the Truth, and by obeying Christ's commandments, we shall bear much fruit. With the power of the Holy Spirit given, all who believe may do all kinds of miraculous things. In Christ, God gives various spiritual gifts to the earthly church, so that the glory of Christ may be revealed. By faith and desire, Christians can experience being poured out and then filled with the Spirit.

We deny the theory that says that wonders, miracles, and the spiritual gifts have been gone since after the apostolic times. Speaking in tongues is not forbidden; nor do we force people to speak in tongues. We don't believe that speaking in tongues is the proof of being saved.

The Church

We believe that the church is formed by the called people whom God has chosen in Jesus Christ. As Christ is the head of the church, the church is the body, the house of God on earth, the pillars and foundation of the Truth. Locally and internationally, the church consists of the global churches with pure and true faith, as well as the churches formed by saints of past generations.

Church administration must be operated according to biblical principles; its work shall not be dominated or controlled by secular rules, but believers must obey the national law. The brethren of the church must take their own duties. By the Spirit, the church ought to be united as one in truth and in Christ.

The mission of the church includes preaching the gospel, teaching, nurturing believers, sending missionaries, reaching those who go astray, and guarding the message of God's truth. The gathering shall not be limited by the number attending or the size of the location. Each believer, as a priest of the Most High, has the responsibility and right to preach the gospel to the ends of the earth.

We oppose the use of the church as a political force.

We disapprove of the church that depends on foreign political support.

We oppose any activities that may destruct the unity of peoples and nations.

The Last Day

We believe that Christ will come again, but no one knows the date except the Father. On that day, Christ is coming on the clouds with mighty angels in glory. Those who have died believing in Christ will rise to life first; then those who are alive at that time will also be changed to be like Him, gathered up in the clouds to meet the Lord.

Whoever does not have their names written in the book of the living will be thrown into the lake of fire. Heaven and earth will be destroyed by fire. Death and the world of the dead will also be thrown into the lake of fire. Those whose names have been written in the book of the living will enter the new heaven and the new earth, and will be with God forever.

While they are waiting for the Lord's return, believers should remain in the Lord's service. Whoever does these things will be rewarded. There are different viewpoints about the tribulation, but a Christian is to keep alert and get ready for the coming of the Lord.

We give thanks and praise to our almighty Father, who has been leading us to complete our faith-confession! May such confession win approval and acceptance. We look forward to seeing more people's hearts strengthened and their faith enlarged. We welcome the bigger revivals of the future.

May the Lord bless the Chinese Church!

May the Lord bless the Chinese people!

Praise, glory, and might be given to the Lord God. Amen!

Dedicated by:
China Gospel Fellowship Representative: Yiping Shen
China Return to the Lord Representative: Rongliang Zhang
China Blessing Church Representative: Xianqi Zheng
Other: Junlv Wang
November 26, 1998

25

The Fellowship of Shared Suffering

After we completed the confession of faith, we posted it on the Internet, and it immediately grabbed international attention. We all signed the document with our real names except for Peter Xu's sister. Peter Xu was not able to attend the meeting, and his sister used an alias to sign the document. The other leaders and I felt that the document had meaning only if we used our real names and took a public stand for the gospel.

Once the document was released, all of us became the top enemies of the Chinese government; but even though we were wanted men, our walk together was closer than ever before. I was also able to connect with the fellowships in Anhui and Wenzhou in ways that I had not been able to before, and even though they had reservations, they soon joined the Sinim Fellowship.

By the fall of 1999, the police were getting closer to catching me again. I was watching every step to make sure that I was being diligent. On August 21, 1999, I was given an invitation to travel to Tanghe County to be with the China Gospel Fellowship. Two well-known Taiwanese pastors, Yabo Xu and Guanqun Li, were traveling into China to teach and to serve the Chinese church, and they would be teaching there. I was excited to join them at the meeting. I knew they would have great insights that would help me in my walk with Christ.

On the morning of the twenty-third, things seemed to be going normally as we all listened to the teaching. I had no cause for worry. However, as the hands of the clock reached twelve and it was almost time for us to break, I heard a loud noise from the back of the room. In a matter of seconds, police officers pushed their way into the meeting and immediately threw each person to the ground. All purses, bags, backpacks, phones, and wallets were confiscated. There were about fifty of us in that room, including myself, the two visiting Taiwanese preachers, and Pastors Yiping, Jianguo, Shuqian, and Xincai.

After we were taken to the police station and interrogated, the prosecution team did not waste any time. The judge sentenced us pastors to three years of hard labor at Tanghe Prison. I had never been to that prison before, but there was some comfort in being there together with my brothers. The bond between the Fangcheng and Tanghe house churches became even closer. Now our relationship was being solidified through common suffering. We rejoiced that we had the privilege to suffer together.

Our bodies were behind bars, confined within the four walls of a concrete cell, but our spirits were free in Christ. We could not help but sing and shout. We had all been in prison before, so this was nothing new to us; we were in no way novices. In fact, we might have known more about prison life than some of the guards. What a joy it was to be in prison for the name of Jesus! During my time in Tanghe Prison, God reminded me of a song that says, "Nothing can separate us from the body of Christ. How beautiful you are—the body of Christ. Wait on the Lord to come back and take us to be with Him in heaven."

Yet while I was in prison rejoicing, my family was being terrorized. The police went to my home in the middle of the night to conduct a surprise search. They treated my wife and children like criminals as they went through the house, rummaging through drawers and beds and throwing items to and fro. After they had searched everywhere and were satisfied that my family didn't have any illegal religious items, they stole whatever they wanted for themselves. During searches, the police often took radios, umbrellas, watches, and the like.

My two young boys had nightmares for years as a result of brutal raids by the police on my house. My wife was always on edge, looking over her shoulder and watching out for the authorities. The very people who were supposed to protect our family and to keep order in our county terrorized and brought fear to the community.

It seemed as if no one was exempt from the persecution. Even though I was public enemy number one, my family suffered in ways that are hard to imagine. My mother was arrested twice and forced to do hard labor during a time in her life when she should have been looking at retirement. Over the years, my wife had also been arrested twice. In 1983, when I was on the run and the police were looking for me but could not find me, they took out their anger on her. She was taken to prison, leaving my two sons without either of their parents for a time. After the boys had grown up, married, had families of their own, and were involved in the work of the church, their wives were arrested and put in jail. These situations were among the hardest trials of my life. Not knowing where your children are laying their heads at night or how your wife is being treated is one of the cruelest punishments that the human mind can endure.

> I was public enemy number one, but my family also suffered in ways that are hard to imagine.

Yet God gave me a wife who has continually amazed me. She is my most valuable treasure. She is such a capable woman. Again, she never asked to marry a Christian, but she has endured the same persecution that I have. For decades, she has suffered, but she has never complained. She never complained when she had to live a life on the run from the police and move from home to home under the cover of darkness. She never complained about our lack of finances or told me fantasies about having wealth. She has always stood by my side and encouraged me to follow the will of God.

In 1981, I had received a letter from an "auntie" (a beloved Christian mentor) in Guangzhou, a city near the coast on the South China Sea, saying that Bibles had just been delivered and that she was making them available to me. My wife was pregnant and was due to give birth to our second child at any time. However, when she heard that there was a unique opportunity to obtain Bibles, she told me to go. She reassured me that she would be fine and that it would be more beneficial for me to get the Bibles than to remain at home for the birth.

When I returned from the trip with the Bibles in hand, my wife had already given birth to our younger son. During my darkest moments in prison, it was always my memories of her that kept me strong in the Lord. She encouraged me and strengthened my faith. Throughout my years in prison, she always visited me on a regular basis wherever visiting was allowed and whenever she was able to. She never forgot a visiting day. She never forgot a holiday or a special occasion. She never forgot to arrange for food, money, or medicine for me.

I have been arrested five times and have spent more than fifteen years in prison altogether. How many periods of fifteen years does one woman have in a lifetime? How can I ever give her back those years? She spent her youth aiding me during my darkest moments. Waiting for her arrival to visit me gave me something to look forward to, but watching her leave always left a void in my heart.

During the years I spent in prison, I was able to sit and meditate on how much my wife really means to me, and I have kept a collection of writings that I composed about her while in prison. Below are a few of the poems I wrote to my wife over those long years of incarceration.

> You have lost so much
> Wandering from place to place.
> We walked on this path of suffering together,
> Yet here we are under the protective wings of the Lord.
> Your love has never been expressed through words,
>   but through your service.
> You sought only peace—but you bore suffering.
> You never rejected suffering
> but accepted it as a gift from the Lord.

...

Your labor in the field was not easy, but done in love.
The plants recognize you,
The flowers smile at you and wave,
The morning birds bid you farewell,
The grain watches as you go by;
They all know that you bring vitality
       and life to them with your sweet labor.

      ...

Millions of people have been blessed by you;
The souls fill the earth from north to south
       because of your labor;
Without you I would have been stuck in prison.
You are the inseparable friend of God.

      ...

From youth to old age you have not stopped sacrificing for me.
Your legs have grown weaker.
Your teeth have become fewer.
Your eyesight has grown dimmer.
Humiliation, mockery,
      and lies fill the memories of your youth.
Never have you given up hope for what lies ahead
      because you know that God is waiting for you
      at the finish line.

After only a few months in prison, I was released in February of 2000 because I had a severe illness that needed treatment.

26

A Visit to America

In 2000, things changed for the Sinim Fellowship. Under a series of persecutions, it seemed that the fellowship was heading toward a dead end. The leaders were either being arrested and thrown into prison or were leaving China altogether. Peter Xu was in prison in Xinxiang, Shen Yiping in Luo Yang, Zhang Xianqi in Bengbu, Zheng Shuqian in Pingdingshan, Miao Zhitong in Wenzhou, and Brother Yun in Burma. Chen Xiao Fu and I were put into Tanghe prison, but we were released earlier than the others.

The government crackdown had wrapped itself around the leadership of the underground house church movement and squeezed us like a python, but we had all been born out of persecution, and in persecution we had learned that God's love for us is one of the few things that never changes. Even when the ever-shifting sands of this world and the false hope of security change, His love for us never does.

I cried out to God, knowing that the church was united in Christ, not in earthly leaders. Even though we leaders had been crushed, beaten down, and thrown into prison, I knew that the body of Christ would not be destroyed. I started to sing a Chinese song that says, "The storms or the consuming fire, no matter how tough the times look, the green grass cannot be destroyed. The green grass will still grow to the ends of the earth."

Those who wait on the Lord in troubled times will be renewed. I did not know it then, but God was bringing the Chinese church to a place where we would see even more unity among believers. Groups that had previously been concerned about joining the Sinim Fellowship put their concerns aside. As I wrote in the previous chapter, the two major groups in Anhui, as well as the churches in Wenzhou, joined hands with us.

The unity that exists among the underground churches in China today came from the Sinim Fellowship. In fact, I attribute the freedoms that Christians experience today in modern China to the efforts put forth by the fellowship. If there had been only five hundred lonely Christians standing together against the efforts of the government, all of them could easily have been wiped out. If there had been five thousand, then perhaps they all would have been incarcerated. But when we came together in fellowship, our numbers were in the millions, so we were far more difficult to destroy.

Sinim Fellowship is not necessarily the name we give to our meetings today, but all of the top leaders come together a couple of times a year under the same bond we formed in the 1990s. The leadership roles rotate, and hosting takes place on a rotation basis, as well. Representatives from Peter Xu's group or Enoch Wang's have not attended since Peter left China, but we continue to congregate, encourage one another, and strategize for the future of the church in China.

In 2000, the Sinim Fellowship was raising awareness of the situation in China among believers internationally, and I began to be invited to speak at churches around the globe. But because of my criminal history, the Chinese government would not issue me a passport to travel abroad. I applied for a passport many times, but no matter how many requests I made, they rejected my applications.

In 2000, due to the movement to modernize China, a way was opened for me to travel outside of the country. Some Chinese cities began to adopt a new policy that would allow them to expand. These cities wanted access to the modernization money that was being used to change the face of China. They would have more of a voice and more access to funds if they were able to acquire a larger geographical area and a larger population. Cities like Zhengzhou were able to expand geographically with little effort, but they needed to persuade more people to move into the city and into the new suburban districts. In an effort to bring in more people, they started a government scheme to allow people to pay a fee to obtain new identification that would permit them to legally live and work in the city.

In the beginning, this new process grew so fast that it did not have the kind of oversight that was customary in the identification alteration process. Members of our church had contacts in the government agencies that were issuing these new identification cards, and I was able to use a fake name to apply for a new residential ID. The cost was only a few hundred renminbi, the equivalent today of between twenty-five and thirty-five U.S. dollars. Once I had the new ID, I was able to apply for a passport using the same alias.

> I felt an obligation to go to the church in America and to thank the believers there for what they had done for my people.

When I applied for my passport in Ximi City, Henan Province, I was not worried that someone would recognize me. Most people were new to the area, like me, and were being issued identification cards that would legally recognize them as residents, which is required in the Chinese Communist system. Without a legal ID, it would not be possible for someone to legally rent an apartment, enroll his children in school, or get a job in an area that was not on his ID. Once I had my new passport, I was immediately able to start traveling. I left China eleven times and visited America, Canada, Australia, Thailand, the Philippines, Egypt, and Jordan.

Before I left for my first trip to America, I reflected on the sacrifices that America, as well as England, had made for my countrymen in the past. Many nations around the world have made sacrifices to bring the gospel to China, but America and England specifically stand out, and I am so very grateful to them. I felt an obligation to go to the church in America and to thank the believers there for what they had done for my people. As a Chinese Christian, I am a recipient of the sacrifices that they have made, and it was my duty to pay my respects. I wanted to give a report to the American churches about the situation in China since the Cultural Revolution. I wanted to give them feedback about the impact of their support, prayers, and sacrifices. And I felt an overwhelming desire to tell them about the amazing revival that we were having.

I traveled to the United States with the songwriter Xiao Min and Sister Ding. As soon as we arrived, we were amazed by all that we saw. The names of the cities that we were traveling to were foreign to me. I could not read the English signs or understand any of the announcements broadcast over the intercom systems at the airports. But I could not wait to go to a real American church. As we traveled around, I was amazed at how many churches there were outside the cities. Even the rural areas had churches that seemingly sprouted up out of the fields.

One of the striking differences I noted between America and China was the impact of nature on American life. I saw Americans eating their food outside, and birds flying around them and eventually landing on the ground and eating only feet away from them. The birds ate beside the Americans without fear. For those who have never visited China, this might seem to be a strange observation, but it was a unique sight to me. You would never see birds trying to eat close to Chinese people who were enjoying their meal—at least not for long. Those birds would quickly end up being part of the meal!

I remember stepping into the first church I visited in America. It was a Pentecostal church, and it seemed that everyone there was white. I had thought that we Chinese were loud and animated when we worshipped Jesus, but we were nothing like that church! Their worship was so loud that I thought I was going to go deaf and would need Jesus to heal my ears before the end of the service.

When they introduced me to speak, an eruption of cheers came roaring up from the crowd. They were so enthusiastic in their warm welcome. A brother from Taiwan came forward to be my translator. I didn't know if he would be able to understand my deep Henan accent, but because he had lived in southern China for a number of years, he was able to adapt to my accent very well. The crowd was visibly alert, listening to every word. It felt strange to be preaching the gospel in America. It felt foreign to be in a place where I could stand on a stage, microphone in hand, and speak without fear of being heard by passersby outside.

I cannot really say how they felt about me or the words that I shared with them except that, after I spoke, they began to pray in response. I was amazed at how passionate their prayers were. The entire congregation really seemed to have a passionate heart for China. After we prayed together, the pastor came forward and talked about the need for finances for ministry in China. Some men came forward, and each of them had a plate in his hand. They began to pass the plates around. I was not sure what they were doing, but after a while I figured out that they were taking up money.

I had never seen an offering take place in this way before. I saw the same thing at every church I went to. After I spoke, an offering plate would be passed around, and the Americans would just freely give their money to help the ministry in China. This practice is completely different from what we do in China. We believe that we should never let the left hand know what the right hand is doing. (See Matthew 6:3–4.) Most of the churches that I worked with were in the countryside. When harvest season came, they would give a tithe according to the harvest. Many of the members would give about twice a year, not on a weekly basis. Most leaders in the Chinese church have about twenty top coworkers who are under them and who represent different cities or provinces throughout the nation. Under those leaders are different counties, and under them are villages. The Chinese believer gives to the church accountant, and the money is distributed upward.

When I first observed the American way of giving, I really thought that their way was wrong. Giving should not be done in the open. However, after my time in America, I began to independently research this American style of giving and have been persuaded that it is biblical. Jesus was able to observe the amount that was given by the widow in the temple. (See Mark 12:41–44; Luke 21:1–4.) Secrecy often gives the devil a foothold with which to attack people who are following Christ. As I reflect on my time in America, I am convinced that Americans are so wealthy because they give so generously.

When I went back to China, I could not wait to return to see my American brothers and sisters again. However, my days of traveling internationally soon came to an end.

27

Under Surveillance

Using a fake name was getting complicated. The postal address for my alias was often identical to that of my real name. There was a dear brother in our church who was a government official, and he freely used his address to collect my mail for me. I had all of my mail sent to him. Then an invitation came to me from a church in America requesting that I come and share with them the amazing things that were happening in China. When the American church mailed the official invitation letter to me, the customs officials scanned the letter and were able to read through the envelope and see that it was an invitation from Christians in the United States.

Customs officials went to the address on the letter and inquired about it. The friend receiving my mail did not know my alias, so when he was asked for whom he was receiving mail, he gave them my real name. With this information, the government quickly deduced that I had been using a fake name and was traveling with a passport by means of an alias.

The police immediately opened up an investigation, knowing that they were after someone who had been playing cat-and-mouse-games with the government for many years. But I had more of an incentive not to get caught than they had to catch me. The police had changed their tactics since the last time I was arrested, and I had changed my evasion techniques to avoid detection. I often stayed in a secret hideout that few people knew about. It was a private apartment in a secluded location on the outskirts of Zhengzhou that was in someone else's name. It was situated in a good place to monitor the surroundings for anyone who might be conducting surveillance over the area.

It didn't take long for me to realize that something was not right. I had a feeling that I was being watched.

I had spent most of my life as a wanted felon, so my list of known accomplices was well-established. One brother who was a trusted colleague didn't know where I lived, but he did know one of my mobile phone numbers. It was a number that I gave only to my closest friends. Somehow, the police got to him. I don't hold anything against him and cannot comment on the conditions he was under when he gave the number to them. He had just been released from prison when he was detained again and questioned about me. Maybe they threatened to throw him back in prison. Maybe he wanted to create good relations with the authorities for future favors. Again, I am not completely sure what circumstances made him give me up, but the police were able to successfully use my cell phone number in their efforts to track me down.

It did not take long for the police to find out where I was, and it didn't take long for me to realize that something was not right. I had a feeling that I was being watched. Having been on the run most of my life, I am often able to distinguish between paranoia and real danger. I set up simple countersurveillance to see if I could detect someone in my area who didn't seem to belong there. When I noticed men watching my window from across the street, I started to suspect that my location had been compromised. Then I saw men walking into my yard systematically and looking into my window. They did this on rotating shifts. At the time, I didn't know exactly why they were watching me, but I knew that I needed to act quickly.

I arranged for a team of men whom I trusted to help me move to a new location. After we had loaded my belongings into a van and driven away, I noticed that a car was following us. We tried to act normally and not do anything that would tip them off to the fact that we knew we were being followed. I prayed that it was only a coincidence that the car was traveling the same route we were.

Once we had arrived at the second apartment, we went inside, and I asked my colleagues to leave two by two. I told them that they had to be careful since we had been followed. After they had all left, I hoped to circumvent whoever was waiting outside. There was only one way to enter and exit the apartment. It was not the best location for slipping out unnoticed, but I had no other choice. As I left the apartment, I tried to keep my head down and remain as inconspicuous as possible. I didn't know the neighbors, and they didn't know me. I was hoping that any stranger I saw would merely be a neighbor I hadn't yet met.

I started to slowly make my way to the street. In my peripheral vision, I saw a man coming toward me. He was wearing plain clothes but was walking with increasing speed and purpose. Then others started to come toward me, and there seemed to be several of them as they closed in. I didn't know who they were, but they obviously knew who I was.

"Zhang Rongliang?" one of the men asked. Before I could fully answer his question, I was engulfed by police officers. They were all wearing plain clothes and shouting obscenities at me. They held me down and searched my body, taking away my phone, my wallet, and everything else I had in my pockets.

"You don't need to use that kind of language," I said as they searched me. "I am a Christian and a believer in Jesus Christ. I prefer that you do not use that kind of language around me." I was surprised at my own behavior. I was not the same person the police had arrested many years ago when I was a young man, and they were not the same young officers who had arrested me. This was a different time and a different China. I had certain rights. The arresting officer did not rebuke me; instead, he apologized to me, and without further communication, the obscenities stopped.

An officer began to scroll through the numbers in the address book of my cell phone. And, before they had even put me in the vehicle, my phone began to ring. Calls were coming in from people who were concerned for my safety. Little did they know that their calls were putting all of us in danger.

I was taken to the police station and questioned, but this time I did not get the beating I was accustomed to. Instead, I underwent an intense barrage of questions, threats, and promises. I don't know if the carrot-and-stick method had ever been used in China before. If it had, I had always gotten only the stick. Whenever a new call would come in to my phone or they had the opportunity to question someone new, the police would return to me with the new evidence and try to make me explain it.

While I was in custody, the police went to my house and found four duplication machines that had been used for mass copying of CDs and VCDs—a video format that was popular in China at that time—for subsequent distribution. They also found memory cards and financial details about the church. My older son had left a memory card in his room that had a lot of information on it. Unfortunately, the information showed where church funds were coming in from and where they were being sent.

My youngest son fled town. On the second day, he escaped to Thailand and from there made his way to the United States. Once I felt secure about his being out of the country, I began to put all the culpability on him.

"How is your son involved?" the police asked me. "We know that he is involved because we have found all these things in his room."

"My oldest son is mentally challenged," I told them. "He has only the capacity to be a driver. He is not mentally capable of doing anything that would be as complex as helping to run a house church network."

Tired from the interrogation, I said that my youngest son was the one whom they wanted to question, that he had helped to direct everything and was basically running the underground house church. After I told them this, they put out a nationwide alert to search for my youngest son, but it was too late. He was already out of the country, and they would never be able to make the arrest. They would be stuck with me alone.

28

On Trial

During the first two months of my imprisonment, I was questioned every day. The questioning was focused entirely on the internal workings of the church. Many of the younger investigators were learning things for the first time. The older members were already well-versed in the inner functioning of the house church.

Even though they knew a lot about it, it was hard for them to imagine why anyone would be so gullible as to join the underground house church movement, so they were continually looking for an angle or an ulterior motive. They were also searching for the magic of my "subversive powers." What made me so special that so many people would join me in an illegal movement and put their lives in danger for what the police perceived to be superstitious nonsense? They thought that perhaps it was money or power, but they never really got the answers they were looking for.

I looked for a glimmer of hope that they would let me go. They continued to threaten me by saying that unless I gave them more information, they would make sure I rotted away in prison. I continued to tell them that they needed to look for my younger son. After two months, I was provided with a lawyer. Unlike my experience in earlier times, I was assigned an attorney who would help me to make a defense and to plead my case before the court. I discovered that the court case would have nothing to do with my role in the underground house church. It would be completely about my having obtained false travel documents. Oddly, during my time in interrogation, I had not been asked about my false identification. My fake ID was of little concern to the authorities during my questioning, but the court case would be exactly the opposite. I was being charged with two separate counts. The first count was for lying on official documents to obtain a fake passport. The second count was for secretly leaving China for subversive activities. I worked with my lawyer for the next six months to prepare a defense. Family and friends prayed for me on a regular basis. Letters and support came in from around the world to petition my case and to plead for my immediate release.

When the court date finally arrived, we were ready to challenge the charges. Before I was taken into the courtroom, the police removed my handcuffs. The court hearing was not held in secret, behind closed doors, but it also had not been released to the media. The information from my case was never given to television stations or newspaper reporters. When I entered the courtroom, I could see that many church members were there, but my family had not been able to attend. Even though we had waited eight months for the trial, the court date had not been set in advance, allowing my family to know when to come. This meant that China could have the trial, make the judgment, and send me off without the inconvenience of having my family members crying and pleading with the court, which might cause observers to have sympathy for my case.

I sat in front of the judge and was ready for my lawyer to present my case. "Zhang Rongliang, you are being charged with two counts. You have been informed of the two counts and have been provided with legal counsel. How do you plead?" the judge asked without emotion. If this was not routine for him, he did not show it. The judge maintained a regal air about him as he presided over the court.

Things had definitely changed since the 1970s and 80s. There was more structure to the proceedings than in the past. The letter of the law had more meaning and carried more weight, which worked in the favor of the defendant. For the past fifty years, China's laws had been enforced with the spirit of the Party members. The commands that they received and carried out had not been written down in any book. They had not been stable enough to be defended against. No law could be referenced that could save you in a room full of Communist accusers. Today, China is learning the lessons of running a more civilized society where law is consistent and people have rights to protect themselves against the actions of the government. It does not always work in the favor of the Christians, of course, but it does balance the scales more than they ever were in the past.

"I plead not guilty."

By the expressions on the faces of the others in the courtroom, my simple statement did not surprise many people. The prosecution was prepared to present its case against me.

My lawyer laid out the defense that we had previously talked about together. He pointed out that my passport was not fake. I had applied for it legally and obtained it legally. The name on the passport was my alias. I had a right to travel to other countries. When I traveled abroad, I did so openly and did not engage in subversive activities. My passport was submitted as evidence to show I had stamps proving that I had exited and reentered China legally. My lawyer pointed out that, previously, I had wrongfully been denied a passport even after I had applied for one many times using my real name.

After hearing my case, the judge was not moved. "Guilty," was his stern verdict. The absoluteness of the moment echoed through the courtroom without fanfare. The ruling was so emotionless that I thought there might be more to it. Maybe the judge was in the middle of his thoughts and would have something to add, but he did not.

Although I was proclaimed guilty, I was not given a sentence. Instead, I was taken back to jail to await sentencing. Soon after I arrived at the jail, I was given a piece of paper, which I held up and read. My crime was spelled out in black-and-white. The familiar Red Star stamp of China with the circle around it glared at me from the bottom of the page, letting me know that this was as official as it

In prison and then out of prison. This relentless cycle was an emotional roller coaster that I was getting too old for.

got. I read through the summary very fast, looking only for the sentence. I found it near the bottom of the page: "For his crimes, Zhang Rongliang is hereby sentenced to eight years."

Eight years, I said to myself. It seemed that the usual cycle of my life was continuing: in prison and then out of prison; on the run and then behind bars again. This relentless cycle was an emotional roller coaster that I was getting too old for. I appealed to the middle courts, but it was of no use. The Chinese authorities wanted me in prison. Arresting me purely for religious activities would have been a public relations nightmare, but I had handed them a golden opportunity. They were able to put me away without ever answering any of the religious rights questions. I was no longer a religious prisoner in their eyes. I was a common criminal who had been apprehended with fake documents that they could prove I had obtained illegally. It was perfect for them if they were ever challenged about my case.

I was sent to Kaifeng Prison in Henan Province. When I walked through the gates, I thought about the Chinese leader Liu Shaoqi, who had died there. Liu Shaoqi is China's forgotten president. Most Westerners and even many Chinese have a misinformed view that Mao Zedong was China's one and only national leader. However, for about ten years, from 1959 to 1969, Liu Shaoqi was China's president. Liu Shaoqi had a different view of the future of China and thus became a political enemy of Mao Zedong. In 1969, he was sent to Kaifeng Prison, where he was repeatedly beaten. He was given no medical care for his diabetes and was eventually found dead, lying on the floor covered in diarrhea and vomit. His body was cremated, and his family was not informed of his death until three years later.

Is this the place where I, too, will die? I asked myself. It was not only possible but probable. Like Liu Shaoqi, I was being brought to Kaifeng Prison as a political prisoner. My health had been deteriorating, and I was not sure how I would handle the hard labor. I had a sinking feeling that I would never leave there alive.

29

Political Prisoner

I was shown my cell in the prison, which I would share with about ten to fourteen people, depending on the time of year. I tried to remain cheerful, but I was not able to summon enough joy to even break a smile. Eight years seemed like a death sentence, and I was certain that I would never see the world beyond those prison walls again. Then, when I was shown the labor that I would be doing in a crude factory setting, I was even more convinced of my fate. My old body would not be able to handle the hard labor any longer. Even the strong young men at the prison strained as they worked the presses at the factory. I noted that bundles of material were being hoisted upon the shoulders of inmates who were only about one third my age. Some of the prisoners were working with heavy material for furniture coverings, using pushing and pulling movements that required the core strength of their bodies. Others were churning out mats that would be used on the floorboards of vehicles. I shook my head at the sight of it.

I can't, I said to myself. *I can't do this.* I was being mentally knocked down before I had even started. *This is surely where I will die. This sweat shop will be the end of me.*

But the Lord spoke to my heart in that low moment, saying, *No. I will not leave you. I will be with you. I will lead you out of here.* The sweet sound of my Father's voice bounced through my soul with warm vibrancy. This was the voice of the heavenly Father who had carried me during the darkest days I have ever experienced in any prison cell. When I was tied up and

The Lord spoke to my heart in that low moment, saying, *I will be with you. I will lead you out of here.*

tortured, His voice had given me strength. When I was hungry and lying on a cold concrete floor without a blanket, His love had brought me warmth. Now, the words of the Father brought me hope, not just because they were comforting but because they were familiar to me.

The familiarity of my Father's voice, which had sustained me over the years, brought nourishment to my soul. With this newfound hope, I knew that I would survive. I had been in much worse situations before. From that point on, I was sure that I would make it out of prison alive.

During the first two months, I was surprised that I was not sent to the factory to work. Instead, I was sent to an education center. Every day, I had to sit on a small stool from 5:00 a.m. until 10:00 p.m. I was forced to sit on that chair with my back straight for the entire day. I was not allowed to do anything other than sit there, and after some time, I could sense the circulation in my legs being cut off. After several hours, my back would begin to scream at me, demanding relief. I wanted to get up, walk around, and stretch out, but I was not allowed to. This was the "education" they gave me.

There was nothing I could do to bring relief to my body, so instead of focusing on my pain, I began to pray. I used the quiet time to get closer to the Lord and to pray about things that I rarely ever thought to pray about. During my time in ministry, I had often found myself busy and active every minute of the day, but now I had nothing to do except talk with my Father. I was able to share all that I had on my heart—including things that I hadn't even known were on my heart.

After the second month, I was sent to work in the factory. I was happy for the change of scenery. But not long after I had reported to the factory for duty, I was sent back to my cell. I thought that maybe I would be brought to the "education" room, but I was not. Confused, I waited to be sent somewhere or to be instructed to do something, but I was not. Everyone else at the prison was working at the factory all day, so I was the sole inmate in my cell, and I was even free to stroll around the garden outside the cell. The authorities had assigned two guards to be with me the entire day. Actually, one was a guard and the other was a fellow prisoner whom the guard had assigned to help watch over me.

I thought that the situation was odd, but I didn't want to question it at first. One of the disadvantages of not working in the factory was that I had no opportunity to reduce my sentence. There was an incentive program connected to the factory work that allowed prisoners to shorten their time in prison. Because I was not allowed to work in the factory, I could not participate in the program. I was told that I would serve my full sentence.

Since I once again found myself with lots of free time on my hands, I used much of the time to pray. I prayed that God would send me a Bible so that I could spend the days digging into His Word. I prayed that God would send me brothers and sisters to fellowship with. I also used the time to get to know the prisoner assigned to watch over me. He was a former policeman whose weapon had accidentally discharged; because of the incident, he had been sentenced to prison for two years. When I asked him why I was not working in the factory with the other prisoners, he told me it was because the prison warden did not want me in with the general population. He knew that I would be preaching the gospel to the other prisoners on a regular basis, and he wanted to keep me as isolated from them as possible. They were learning. However, I was able to spend long days talking to the former policeman about Jesus, and he was the first person I led to Christ in Kaifeng Prison.

I started to enjoy my quiet time in the cell every day. Not only would I pace around and pray, but I would also softly sing to myself. And, as I learned more about my cellmates, I was able to pray for them individually. These men were from different walks of life. I was curious about them and wanted to know what they had done to end up in prison. They were curious about me, as well. They were all younger than I, and they referred to me as "the old man." They knew that I was willing to work in the factory but that the prison officials prohibited it. They all wanted to see what kind of person I was that the officials were too scared to allow me to mingle with them.

After I had been at the prison for a while, I was able to establish a daily routine that helped keep me sane. I would wake up every morning at about four. Everyone had to be up by 6:00 a.m., but I wanted to wake up two hours earlier so that I could go for a jog, pray, and clean up before everyone else woke up. Once the rest of the prisoners were up, we would all go to breakfast together at 6:30. Following breakfast, everyone except for me would head off to work at the factory. After they left, I would walk around the yard and meditate, pray, and praise God.

I would break for lunch at noon and then continue the same activities until dinner. The other prisoners would have lunch and dinner at the factory. After dinner, the prisoners would return to their cells. They would watch television and socialize with one another until about nine o'clock. My cellmates were not only curious about me but also wary. They had been told to watch me because I was mentally unstable, even insane. If they were not careful, they would fall subject to my lunacy and become Christians. I think that might actually have increased their curiosity rather than discouraging it.

If I was mentally unstable, I was certainly in good company. Among my fellow prisoners were many drug dealers. There were also a murderer, a thief, and a kidnapper. Another had been convicted of putting poison in food. I was happy that he and I generally ate in different places!

Some of the prisoners were easy to get along with. However, the one who had been convicted of murder and the one who had been convicted of robbery were violent men. They often fought or threatened violence if they did not get their way. Frequently, there were fierce fights in our cell, especially when it was time for the lights to be turned off. The lights were switched off at 9:00 p.m., but some of my cellmates wanted to continue talking afterward. Often, the conversation among certain cellmates got loud, annoying the others who wanted to sleep. This would result in fistfights where blood would be splattered on the floor. That was one of the things that made this time in prison different. Instead of the prison guards drawing blood by beating the prisoners, the prisoners did it to each other.

Previously, my main nemeses had been the prison guards, but this time, I really had to watch my step around my fellow inmates.

By God's grace, I was able to build a relationship with each one of my cellmates and explain the gospel of Jesus Christ to him. Even though this was something the authorities wanted to prevent, I still found a way to share with the other

I was able to build a relationship with each one of my cellmates and explain the gospel of Jesus Christ to him.

prisoners. After a short amount of time and only a little bit of contact, I was able to talk about Jesus with a prisoner who used to be a political official in the Chinese government. When he became ill and was not able to work, I saw it as an open door to share the gospel with him—and I went for it.

This young man was not able to get up and move around. His body was worn out, and he was lying in bed, very weak. However, his mind was obviously active. I approached with both caution and excitement. I did not have many opportunities to share about Jesus with fellow prisoners, and I felt a surge of adrenaline whenever I did. When I asked him if I could tell him about Jesus, he agreed. He soon accepted Jesus as his Lord and Savior.

He had been depressed because of how far he had fallen in life, but before that day was over, he was rejoicing. Though prison was not a place he had ever wanted to be, it was due to his time in prison that he was able to learn about Jesus Christ and receive eternal life. When I'd been out of prison, government officials had been hunting me or watching my every move; but inside this prison, the government officials were open to evangelism. It was a unique opportunity that I never could have found anywhere else.

Another government official who worked at the prison had a wife who was a Christian, and she had heard about me. I was able to share the gospel with him, as well. One night, under the cover of darkness, he put his career on the line to bring me a Bible, which was still considered to be contraband in Chinese prisons. That Bible became my most valued possession. I was able to spend the long days reading it and meditating on its words.

Within a short time, I saw several people come to Christ, even though my exposure to the general population was limited. I was able to have visitors, and I requested that they bring me apples and a basin to wash them in. The main purpose for the wash basin was actually to perform baptisms in the prison. I used it secretly on several occasions.

It was not easy to find opportunities to meet with the new believers after they received Christ, but we were able to arrange to see each other by independently going to the prison clinic to be treated for a "cold," a "sore throat," a "stomachache," or some other manufactured ailment. There were about five thousand prisoners at Kaifeng, and the clinics were busy enough to allow us a few moments together to share Bible verses or words of encouragement as we waited to see the doctor. During Christmastime, the clinic was the busiest, because all the Christians would try to meet up there. We thought up various conditions that would require us to see the doctor, seizing an opportunity to celebrate the birth of our Savior together.

Life at Kaifeng Prison had begun to become routine for me, but this would soon change.

30

Stroke!

My daily life was pretty relaxed considering I was a prisoner. I fell into a pattern that helped pass the hours and days. The days kept going by; they turned into weeks and then months. The weather changed back and forth from hot to cold as the seasons passed by in slow motion.

None of my memories of the times I spent in the prison garden really stand out against the backdrop of my years in prison. They have all meshed into one continual memory. Prison life had a monotony about it that rivaled the burdens of hardship. The isolation from my family, my friends, and my fellowships took a toll of its own. Prison stole time that could never be replaced.

Then, on July 1, 2007, the monotony of my prison life was shattered. The morning had started off as usual when I woke up at four. After breakfast, I began walking around the prison yard. But as I walked, I felt something strange in my right foot. It was tingling and going numb at the same time. I lifted it off the ground and put it back down again. Everything looked normal, but something was not right. With all the times that my legs and feet had gone numb over the years after being forced into the most torturous positions, it was a strange sensation to experience numbness when I was walking normally.

The numbness quickly spread to the entire right side of my body until I was no longer able to walk. In the middle of the prison yard, I crumpled to the ground and was unable to pick myself back up. As I fell to the ground,

I was reminded again of Liu Shaoqi, who had died in Kaifeng Prison from lack of medical care. Would I follow in his path? With everyone else at the factory all day, and with the mediocre care at the prison, how would I fare? I called out to the Lord, who was my only salvation.

Virtually every prisoner who'd had a stroke in Kaifeng Prison had died; my odds of survival were therefore not very high.

I saw one of the prisoners charged with keeping an eye on me. I was able to get his attention and yelled out to him that I couldn't walk and needed emergency help. The prison guard was not there, so the man went to find him. The entire right side of my body went limp and had no feeling. What an odd sensation it was to have half my body die on me. Although I could see that side of my body, I couldn't feel it at all. My right side was like a foreign appendage clipped on to me but somehow detached from everything else. It was clear that I was having a stroke. Virtually every prisoner who'd had a stroke in Kaifeng Prison had died; my odds of survival were therefore not very high. But I was rushed to the prison hospital and taken to one of the six small inpatient rooms, where the staff immediately began to treat me. I silently called out to the Lord for help.

For the next two months, I received physical therapy. The hospital personnel gave me every kind of medicine they could, but in the beginning, I was completely immobile. The prison did not have a big budget to supply the proper medication for prisoners, so the medicine they were giving me did not hold much promise.

At first, I was not able to walk or even use the restroom without assistance. Most people believed that I would be handicapped for the rest of my life; but due to much prayer, my family was able to obtain medication from international sources to treat the symptoms. After a month of taking the new medication, I was able to walk again.

The staff members at the prison hospital were very invested in my situation and were watching my every movement. Most of them had expected me to die on the day I was admitted; instead, I was on the road to a miraculous recovery. Again, things were far different at Kaifeng from my previous four experiences in prison. The medical care had improved significantly. There was a genuine attempt to keep me as healthy as possible, in contrast to when I had been beaten on a regular basis. In 1976, the prison guards had not been concerned about the loss of my life. In fact, they most likely would have welcomed it. Today, the guards are held responsible for the well-being of their prisoners.

In the 1970s, there had been barely any food to eat, but at Kaifeng, we were provided with three meals a day. The majority of prisoners I had served with in the past had been political prisoners, but today the prison system is mostly reserved for genuinely hardened criminals guilty of theft, drug dealing, or murder.

During my earlier years in prison, I had not be able to obtain the basic necessities for mere survival, but the Kaifeng Prison had a small store where a wide variety of comfort items could be purchased. Prisoners were also free to play games, talk, and watch television. They didn't always get to do this, of course, because of the labor they had to do every day, but things had definitely taken a turn in the right direction, although there are exceptions.

During 2006, the year before my stroke, prison officials had given me pen and paper and instructed me to write out a confession that I was the leader of a cult. I was told that the prison would reduce my sentence if I wrote the letter. Without even thinking about it, I became verbally combative and responded that I could not write such a letter. "How am I a cult leader?" I asked. "What I believe is the same as what most Christians around the world believe. Most of the people in America and Europe—even some of their leaders—believe the very things I believe." At any other time in the last sixty years in China, my refusal to write a confession would have earned me a very thorough beating. However, the social weather in China was changing. The prison officials took their pen and paper, walked away, and never bothered me again with the idea of a confession.

After the stroke, I was allowed to be visited only by my wife and one of my sisters. In addition, my oldest son had taken over the daily duties of running the network, and the police wanted to arrest him. When I was discharged from the hospital and returned to my room to rejoin the general population, I resumed my daily schedule of praying, reading my Bible, and preaching the gospel to all those around me. I didn't realize that my days at the prison were coming to a close.

31

"Don't You Want to Go?"

Out of the entire population of five thousand prisoners, only a small percentage of the men had actually become Christians. I wanted to have more time with each of them to proclaim the good news of Jesus Christ that could change them in spite of their situation. I wanted to introduce them to the Redeemer who had set me free from the chains of anger, despair, and death so many years earlier. Not everyone liked my message. Some of the prisoners would mock me for my beliefs, but I shared with them nonetheless.

My Bible became the centerpiece of the small Christian fellowship that we formed. It was such a blessing to have a Bible with which to conduct services and ceremonies inside the prison. Every prisoner had a small locker in which he was permitted to keep his belongings and his hygiene items. I often kept my Bible in mine. Sometimes, I would strap it to the bottom of my bunk with tape so that it would not be found. Other times, I had friends hold it for me during inspections so that the authorities would not be able to find it. The prison officials would conduct surprise searches, but they never were able to find my Bible or take it away from me. My Bible stayed with me until I left the prison.

At the end of 2010, an official called out my name and announced that I would be set free nine months earlier than my scheduled release date. He told me that the officials had discussed my situation and decided that I should be released early because of my health condition. After I heard this news, I started to make my rounds and prepare all of the brothers for my upcoming departure. I appointed leaders for the small cell groups and discipled them on how to lead. I taught intensive evangelism classes to prepare them for sharing the gospel with other prisoners after I left. I had them commit to Bible verse memorization and showed them how to search the Bible for the answers they needed.

When we prayed together, I looked at each one of them while their eyes were closed, knowing that it would not be easy to leave them behind. These brothers had been such a large part of my life during my seven years in Kaifeng Prison. I spent Chinese New Year with them every year. They had helped me through the tough trials of recovery after my stroke. We were close now, and it would be hard to say good-bye. Many of them would never see the outside of Kaifeng Prison again, but they would see paradise and live for eternity with our Father.

When you read only one book day after day, it will leave more than an impression. And when that book is the Word of God, it will transform your life.

I took the Bible I had carried during many of my years at the prison, ran my fingers along its edges, and thought of all the good memories connected with it. I remembered the hours I'd spent pacing the prison yard while praying and reading that Bible. Any book you read can leave an impression on you, but when you read only one book day after day and hour after hour, it will leave more than an impression. And when that book is the Word of God, it will transform your life. I had built a relationship with that Bible. I could visualize where certain Scriptures were located within its pages—I could even see in my mind's eye on which side of the page they were printed—Scriptures that had carried me through some trying times.

While that Bible had helped me through those difficult times, it was not meant to leave the prison with me. I handed it over to one of the inmates who was leading a cell group fellowship. I had never owned the Bible. I had possessed it for only a short while; but, like a river, its words had flowed into my heart, changed my life one word at a time, and then flowed into the lives of others as I shared them.

I was unable to sleep on my final night in prison. I sat up in my bed from midnight onward. I counted the minutes until 9:00 a.m. because I knew that around that time a prison guard would bring me my release papers, and I would have my ticket to freedom. My mind rushed with images of sleeping in my own bed in my own home and waking up next to my wife instead of in a roomful of convicts.

Morning finally came, and I got up, showered, and changed out of my blue prison uniform. I prayed that it would be the last time I would ever again have to see that blue jumpsuit, with its black-and-white-striped pockets. After I received my papers, an officer whom I had gotten to know led me out of the prison. I was walking behind him, but he did not hear my footsteps tracing so closely behind his, and when he turned toward me, he was shocked to see me so near to him. He opened the gate and motioned for me to walk through, but I paused.

"What are you doing? Come on, let's go," he said while motioning with his hand for me to exit the prison. "What's the matter?"

I didn't respond.

"Don't you want to go?" he asked.

"No." I was surprised at my own words. They spoke a deep truth that welled up from inside me, one that I had not even realized was there. "No. I do not want to leave," I reiterated with no less surprise the second time.

He lowered his head as he looked at me, and in a very serious, fatherly tone that held an inflection of care, he said, "Please go, and don't ever come back to this place."

I turned to look at the prison, and I saw many of my friends waving at me. Some of them had grabbed their towels and were flapping them in the air in farewell. A few prisoners had even run back inside to grab the sheets off their beds and then come back to their windows to wave them at me. I couldn't help but feel love and compassion for those whom I was leaving behind. The Spirit of the Lord came upon me, and I could hear Him say, *Just as you sent men and women to preach the gospel in the far-flung provinces of China, Asia, and the Middle East, so have I sent you to preach the gospel to the prisoners of Kaifeng.*

I had never been alone. God had been with me every step of the way, providing comfort and power.

The words of the Lord stunned me, freezing me in place. It had been no easier for the young missionaries who had gone into foreign lands to preach the gospel to the lost than it had been for me to be sent to Kaifeng Prison. And I had never been alone. God had been with me every step of the way, providing comfort and power. Being in Kaifeng had not been about me. It had been about God.

I am crucified with Christ, and it is no longer I who live but He who lives in me. (See Galatians 2:20.) I had kept thinking of my journey in prison as a personal trial to make me stronger. I had seen the trials as God's way of bringing *me* closer to Him. Yet, standing there and watching all those enthusiastic young men waving to me as I was about to leave, I realized how selfish those thoughts had been. No, it was not about me at all—it was about them, and, ultimately, it was about God's glory. It was about God's love being known to all men—even those at Kaifeng Prison—for His glory alone.

The trial had not been easy, but I would not trade those seven years. Shadrach, Meshach, and Abednego had been thrown into the fiery furnace. That furnace had been blazingly hot, but they had not been burned up. Not only had they not been burned, but they had also walked around joyfully in the midst of the flames! (See Daniel 3.)

With those thoughts, I turned and walked out of Kaifeng Prison.

32

The Story of China

After having been in prison for seven years, I thought I would return to a church that was in complete disarray, but that was not the case. It seems that God's church moves forward with or without us. It is not a privilege for God to have us serve Him—the privilege is all ours. My oldest son had been running things for the past seven years while I was incarcerated, and the church had continued to grow exponentially.

The church had stood beside our family throughout the entire time I was in prison. Brothers and sisters never once stopped looking after my wife and taking care of her needs. During those seven years, it had become more and more difficult for her to travel from our hometown to Kaifeng for visits, so she had moved to Zhengzhou in order to be closer to the prison. She was not able to get a regular job because of her connection to me. In our hometown, we'd owned chickens and pigs, and she had been able to raise them as a means to support our family. She had run the farm, taken the goods to the market, and sold them to the various merchants. However, when she moved to the large metropolitan city of Zhengzhou, she was no longer able to do any of those things, and she had to rely on others for help. All of the aid and provision we received from so many brothers and sisters was an amazing blessing that I will never be able to pay back.

In Chinese culture, it is customary for the sons of a family to look out for the financial situation of their parents, but our younger son had fled to America, and our older son was on the run in China and unable to visit, call, or otherwise communicate with us. The support that we received from brothers and sisters around the world helped in ways that I don't think they will ever know this side of heaven.

Although we continue to be able to survive financially in China, it is difficult to explain the dark abyss that exists in our lives knowing that somewhere in the world we have three beautiful grandchildren growing up whom we are not able to be with. Our younger son has two children, a son and a daughter, and our older son has a baby boy. Whenever the holidays come around, the loneliness of not being around our three grandchildren is deafening, and it grows only louder and more painful with age. There are few things that make growing older sweeter than having grandchildren. Conversely, few things can bring more pain than being separated from them and knowing that they will never really know who you are.

◡‿

My story is not just the story of Chinese Christians—it is the story of China. My life—growing up as a peasant farmer, joining the Communist Party, and then suffering for the kingdom—runs parallel to the last seventy years of Chinese history. China was a country of postwar peasants who embraced Communism, and for the last several decades, she has been searching for her spiritual soul.

For the last several decades, China has been searching for her spiritual soul.

I have never been an enemy of the Chinese people, something I have been repeatedly accused of. On the contrary, I love my country. I have always longed for China to love me as much as I love her. Jesus died for the Chinese people, and He has called me and many others to do the same. When Jesus hung on the cross, He said about His executioners, *"Father, forgive them, for they know not what they do"* (Luke 23:34). We could say the same about China. She persecuted Christians in the blindness of sin.

I believe that one day very soon, things will be different for Christians in China. The nation is changing every day at a rate that is hard to keep up with. If I were to give a status report today about the situation in China, it would most likely change before the publication of this book. I am more excited today about China than I have ever been before. We are seeing one of the biggest revivals in the world, with several thousand people coming to Christ every single day. Many of those who are becoming Christians are government officials, and this is having a huge impact.

I attended a fellowship meeting just the other day and was amused at the young ladies who came to church wearing high heels. Of course, the young women had no idea that I was noticing their footwear. They also would not know that it hadn't been possible for women to wear high heels only twenty years ago, because everyone had to be prepared to run if the police stormed into a meeting. The believers in the fellowship I attended did not seem the least bit worried about being raided. They were not looking over their shoulders, waiting for an impending police incursion. They were simply lost in praise and worship.

Many Westerners and other foreign observers are pushing—and praying—for the underground church to register with the Chinese government, as other "official" churches in China have, but that day has not yet come. As things stand today, it is still impossible due to the scars of past betrayals, as well as ongoing concerns about compromise. However, the house church is more openly active than it has ever been. This trend will only continue, and I believe that the growth will be in harmony with the growth of China as it continues to open up to the world.

As China proceeds to grow economically, politically, and militarily, it is also growing spiritually. As a people, we are marching out of the black void of atheism and into the destiny of our Creator. Today, "Back to Jerusalem" is the heartbeat of the Chinese church's vision for the future, which is the vision to take the gospel of Jesus Christ from the borders of China into the poorest, darkest, most violent areas on earth until Jesus' Great Commission is fulfilled and every tribe, tongue, and nation has heard the good news.

When I was a young believer being tortured in prison, our church was begging Jesus to help us survive; but mere survival is blasphemy. We have been called to do more than simply survive. During the times I was imprisoned and fearing for my life, Jesus was not scared that His kingdom in China was falling apart. He was using the stumbling block of the enemy as a stepping-stone for His servants. The church in China did not crumble under persecution—it thrived. It didn't grow in spite of suffering—it grew because of it. God's plan for China did not have to adjust and shift to emergency mode due to the policies of Mao Zedong; His plan included Mao Zedong all along.

> **The church in China did not crumble under persecution— it thrived. It didn't grow in spite of suffering—it grew because of it.**

Today, the underground house churches in China are not trying to survive. They are unified in the Back to Jerusalem vision, and churches are sending out missionaries into Muslim, Buddhist, Hindu, and atheist countries around the world. Our church now has missionaries serving in Pakistan, Dubai, India, and many other nations that are hostile to the gospel. Additionally, our young people are moving into China's cities in large numbers, but it is not for the purpose of making money. They are moving there to plant churches, to preach the gospel, to raise support for foreign missions, and to send new firebrand believers into the field. I can't help but feel excited about the future of China and the Chinese church.

China is my home. It is the country of my birth, and I have never tried to escape from it. Since my release from prison, the police have regularly called me and checked up on me. They want to know where I am and what I am doing. It's hard to imagine, but the police officers and I have actually grown old together. Many of the officers have been chasing me their entire careers. They have seen me arrested and thrown into prison again and again. They will never know the love that I have for them and the desire that I have for them to find eternal life.

While I was preparing this book, one of the chief officers in the Zhengzhou police department asked me to dinner with him and some of the other police officers. I knew they had been listening to my phone conversations. And I knew that *they* knew I knew this. It was the unspoken, open secret at the table as we ate together. Before we began, I asked everyone to pause as I said a blessing over the meal. Our years of cat-and-mouse had earned me the respect of silence as I said grace and prayed a blessing over the food, over China, and over each of the officers seated around that table. They may not know it, but those words will penetrate the depths of their hearts far beyond that meal; and I believe that the Father will provide supernatural protection over them as they do their jobs and that one day that hedge of protection will be revealed to them in a most spectacular way.

After the prayer, the main police chief leaned in toward me as if he had something important to communicate. "You know, Zhang, it would be interesting if you wrote a book about your life one day," he said to me in a bit of a cheeky manner. He was hinting at the fact that he knew what I had been up to. "If you do write a book, what would you say? You are not getting any younger, you know...." He paused for effect before concluding, "...and it would be a shame to see you arrested again."

I don't know if my book will ever be distributed in China, but if it ever is, I would like to give the first copies to my dear old friends in the police department.

EPILOGUE:

Streams from the River

I have been in prison, I have been beaten to a bloody pulp, and I have been tortured numerous times. I have gone days without food until my stomach felt like it was turning inside out from cramps, and I have gone without water until my tongue felt like a dry desert. I know all too well what poverty feels like; there were times when I did not have two coins to rub together. Yet those trials of prison, torture, hunger, thirst, and poverty pale in comparison to the hardest trial I have ever gone through in my entire life.

Being rejected by the world for the name of Jesus Christ is a biblical guarantee that comes again and again like a revolving door, and it should not be a surprise to us when it happens. Even though the trials of this world have been a challenge for me both physically and spiritually, I have found comfort in the knowledge that Jesus has never left me. I have also found strength in the brothers and sisters whom He has sent to be with me.

However, the most daunting, bone-shaking trial I have ever endured was not at the hands of my enemies but at the hands of my brothers in Christ. In 2003, many difficulties arose between my coworkers and me. These were the top leaders who oversaw various geographical areas of ministry and who were my close colleagues—and I was their pastor. It is not easy to point to just one problem that led to the difficulties; indeed, it was a culmination of several things. After we had endured years in which all of us were on the run, tensions sometimes ran high; miscommunication was often more common than correct communication, and there was even a misunderstanding of intentions.

I was not blameless; my hands were not clean. None of the problems we were having had really been dealt with. They ran under the surface, and they were growing more and more noticeable during our times of worship together. The discord in our group was almost tangible at times. It filled the air and choked everyone in its path. The sweet incense of praise was being snuffed out by the ugly stench of conflict. I was losing hold of my relationships with my dear coworkers.

As a pastor, I felt that I should be able to just command unity to appear. I expected that I could tell everyone to get over their problems and move on and that would be the end of it, but it was not so easy. I became increasingly frustrated with my lack of authority over the situation. After only a short while, I became easily irritable and prone to aggressive outbursts of anger, which only escalated the situation and widened the gap between my coworkers and me.

In the early days, we didn't have time for discord. We were involved in trench warfare together and were united in heart. We were arrested together and tortured together. We shared the same prison cells and counted it all joy to suffer for Jesus' name. But as things eased up and we saw more finances come into the church, a demon emerged that we had never tackled. Issues regarding the handling of money, chains of command, responsibilities and duties, and leadership roles were the new problems we were dealing with. Again, I was the pastor, and I felt that was enough. I thought I should be able to give the orders as they were to be carried out and the discussion would be over.

Each one of these problems festered in our wounded hearts. Even though we tried to deal with them in what we considered to be a Christian way by overlooking them, they would not be so easily ignored. They kept slowly biting at us over and over again until the small problems became a massive dragon that refused to be slain.

I was not easily going to admit defeat. I held on to hope that the winds of discontent would soon blow over. Maybe if we were all arrested and thrown into prison again, these problems would just disappear; but no police came, and there was no prison cell to be had for our weary souls.

By Chinese New Year 2003, the leadership of the Fangcheng Network was in full revolt. Our issues had snowballed, and it seemed inevitable that five of the main leaders I had trusted in were ready to do the unthinkable—to split off from Fangcheng. As their friend, as their brother—as their pastor—I felt betrayed. The anguish that it caused me was no small matter. I would rather have been strapped into a chair and beaten by a muscle-bound prison guard than see the church divided. I had reached the end of my rope and was all out of ideas, so I called Brother Ren.

Brother Ren is an old friend of mine from Scandinavia. From the early days, he used to spend time with us in the rural areas, preaching the gospel to us and systematically teaching the leaders of the underground house church. All the leaders in China respected and admired him. Even though my close brothers did not want to discuss matters with me, I knew that they would sit down and talk with Brother Ren.

As Chinese New Year drew closer, I knew that everyone would want to return home and spend the holidays with their families, but I had no time to waste, so I arranged for us to meet with Brother Ren. My coworkers were my family, and I could not imagine enjoying the holidays if they were no longer walking the same path together with me. Brother Ren is a natural mediator. Whenever he enters a room, his presence ushers in a peaceful, calm atmosphere. He greeted each of us with a long hug, a warm smile, and eye contact that told us that everything was going to be all right because the Lord was in control.

I was ready to do anything to keep our church from splitting, and I needed Brother Ren to just sprinkle some magic dust on our situation and make it all better. I imagined an ending that resulted in all of us hugging, crying, asking for forgiveness, and then moving on. In my mind, Brother Ren was like a mechanic. He would just find the broken part of the car and fix it, and then we could keep on driving.

First, Brother Ren and I met together and openly discussed the problems that we were experiencing, how to approach everything with the younger leadership, and how to propose a solution. He went and spoke with the brothers, but they did not agree with the solution. It was clear that they had made up their minds. When Brother Ren came to me and tried to explain the situation, I was infuriated. I could not believe this was happening. We had been through so much together and had come out on the other side because of the glory of the Lord. After all the trials and tribulations that our underground house church network had suffered, the entire Communist Party of China had not been able to break us or to split us up. But now, inconceivably, a split seemed to be happening.

I just could not grasp the reality of the situation. It was as if the world was spinning all around me. Everything that I thought I had learned from years of persecution was being turned inside out. I was upset with everyone. I really felt that my church was falling apart. Later, I would understand that it was not my church but God's church. The idea of "my" church was blasphemous.

One person who had the understanding to help me through this difficult season was Brother Yun, "the Heavenly Man." He had patience when mine had run out. He had understanding when I thought that things were completely incomprehensible. God used Brother Yun, with his love and his humbleness, to help me through those hard times. I will never forget his devotion to me during those years.

A verse from Psalm 46 came to me one day and gave me joy after the tempest had calmed. It says, *"There is a river, the streams whereof shall make glad the city of God, the holy place of the tabernacles of the most High"* (Psalm 46:4 KJV). When a river splits into streams, it does not necessarily seem like a desirable thing. Mother river carves her path but cannot dictate the direction of the streams that break off from her. Yet it is necessary that those streams break off in order to bring nourishment to the dry lands that are far from the river.

I had desperately wanted to keep us all in the same network, but because God had His way instead of me having mine, there are people today who are part of the church who might never have come to Christ because the river would have been too far removed from their lives. The church in China today is God's making! His ways are so much bigger than my ways, and He creates testimonies in the midst of every trial.

China is huge, with a population of more than 1.4 billion people. Even all five of the major house church networks combined were never going to be able to facilitate the work that needed to be done. In the past, I'd wanted so dearly to hold on to those five networks as I had known them. But today I pray that God will raise up a million different networks to carry out the work of His kingdom. All glory be to God!

About the Authors

Zhang Rongliang has been a leader of the Fangcheng House Church (also called "China for Christ Church") in Henan Province, China, for thirty years. He has been persecuted and tortured, and has spent approximately a quarter of his life in prison. Today, Zhang continues to lead, inspire, and disciple within Fangcheng.

⌒

Eugene Bach is a pseudonym for a member of the Chinese underground church who does not wish to be identified. He has been working with underground churches in China for more than fifteen years, helping their members to establish forward mission bases in closed countries around the world, including Iraq and Syria. Eugene leads the Chinese mission movement called Back to Jerusalem, which provides essential support for Chinese missionaries in Africa, Asia, and the Middle East. He has written books about the underground church in China, North Korea, and Iran.

Welcome to Our House!

We Have a Special Gift for You

It is our privilege and pleasure to share in your love of Christian books. We are committed to bringing you authors and books that feed, challenge, and enrich your faith.

To show our appreciation, we invite you to sign up to receive a specially selected **Reader Appreciation Gift**, with our compliments. Just go to the Web address at the bottom of this page.

God bless you as you seek a deeper walk with Him!

WE HAVE A GIFT FOR YOU. VISIT:

whpub.me/nonfictionthx

WHITAKER
HOUSE